MARTIN CLASSICAL LECTURES

These lectures are delivered annually at

OBERLIN COLLEGE

on a Foundation established in honor of

CHARLES BEEBE MARTIN

They are published for Oberlin College by the

HARVARD UNIVERSITY PRESS

LONDON : HUMPHREY MILFORD

OXFORD UNIVERSITY PRESS

ASPECTS OF SOCIAL BEHAVIOR IN ANCIENT ROME

MARTIN CLASSICAL LECTURES
VOLUME II

BY TENNEY FRANK

PROFESSOR OF LATIN IN THE JOHNS HOPKINS UNIVERSITY

CAMBRIDGE : MASSACHUSETTS

HARVARD UNIVERSITY PRESS

1932

PRINTED AT THE HARVARD UNIVERSITY PRESS
CAMBRIDGE, MASS., U. S. A.

THE MARTIN CLASSICAL LECTURES

VOLUME II

THE Martin Foundation, on which these lectures
are delivered, was established by his many friends
in honor of Charles Beebe Martin, for forty-five
years a teacher of classical literature and
classical art in Oberlin College

FOREWORD

THE student of Greek sociology has at his disposal — besides the standard histories — the incomparable picture of early civilization in Homer's epics, the realistic comedies of Aristophanes and Menander with their penetrating interpretation of contemporary Greek life, a large number of pleas delivered in private lawsuits, and much informative occasional literature that survived because of the long life of the Eastern empire. The Latinist fares less well. From the early days of Rome we have only a few pages of legal fragments. Epic poets of a later day — from whom Livy drew his conceptions of early civilization — attempted to restore the outlines of primitive Rome, but the legends with which they worked had already taken on much sophistication before they were recorded. The hundreds of plays that truly reflected actual life at Rome have all been lost; the only plays that survive are the Plautine and Terentian paraphrases of Greek plays. The speeches of Cicero that remain deal largely with political matters. Indeed a very small fragment of republican literature — perhaps not over a twentieth part — survived the fall of Rome: the monks of the Middle Ages who sifted out what they needed possessed rather narrow interests. The great source-book of the student of Roman society is, of course, the collection of some 900 of Cicero's letters, about one fourth of the original mass. This is priceless material, but it covers a relatively brief period. The works of Petronius and Apuleius may almost be termed sociological novels, but they, too, afford only hasty glimpses into important epochs. For our materials we have to read endlessly in the works of political-minded historians, of moralizing essayists, of bitter satirists, to delve in legal codes, in tantalizing papyri and inscriptions, and even in poetry, for the infrequent phrases that throw faint shimmers of light on our problems. We shall probably never have adequate sources for a well-rounded work on Roman sociology.

One of the difficulties in an attempt to characterize Roman society is the paradoxical fact that the Romans in Cicero's day were so like the modern man that one is apt to miss necessary distinctions. In reading the letters of Cicero we soon reach the conviction that if he could return to us as a guest we could live with him with almost the same degree of mutual comprehension as with any foreigner of our own time. If he spoke our language and assumed our dress, we should soon be oblivious of the twenty centuries that separate us. We should easily agree in matters of politics, of art, and literature; he would find little that was unfamiliar in our home life and in our social gatherings; our religion might seem strange to him, but not the moral code connected with it; in points of human etiquette we might have to guard ourselves in order not to surprise his delicate sense of the fitting. In other words, we should never have occasion to assume from such a contact that human nature had changed in any essential these two thousand years. It is only in the externals of a few social conventions, some religious formalities, some customs of political procedure, and a few artistic practices that we should have to make slight adjustments in our conversation. And in these matters Cicero would as frequently feel surprise at our subjection to unnatural conventions as we should at his behavior.

The differences are on the whole merely external, and yet in their social consequences these are very real. In family organization the Romans lived in the shadow of an attenuating patriarchal system; we dwell rather within the penumbra of forms imposed by a universal church. The institution of slavery left consequences more serious to Roman society than to ours because there slavery had proceeded to the point of checking salutary industries, and lack of racial prejudice had permitted a more active absorption of indigestible foreign elements in the body politic. Then again an over-rapid territorial expansion at Rome encouraged the growth of an agrarian-military régime in the state which in time imposed an autocracy that precluded the development of a healthy participation of all citizens in political life and thought. And finally, as a result of slavery and expansion, a host of strange religious cults permeated the Roman Empire that eventually weaned the citizens away from habits of self-reliance into those of intellectual subservience.

In these lectures I have selected for discussion a few of the topics in which Roman society seems to me to deserve further consideration, and I have not wholly shunned the temptation of discussing various points that are still *sub judice*, for the students of Oberlin College are well trained in the use of primary sources. However, the chief purpose of the course was to provide a general conspectus of each topic rather than to delve into the minutiae of personal investigations. I have also added some notes at the end, not only to suggest further reading, but also to afford a buttress to some heterodox opinions.

T. F.

April 6, 1931

CONTENTS

ASPECTS OF SOCIAL BEHAVIOR
IN ANCIENT ROME

I

THE ROMAN FAMILY

WHEN Roman writers began to compare their own social customs with those of the Greeks they were struck especially by the differences in the position of women in the Greek and Roman households. Cornelius Nepos admits in the preface of his *Lives* that he hesitates to mention some of the acts of Greek generals recorded in his book because to Roman readers they may seem trivial. Then he adds:

On the other hand, many actions are seemly according to our code which the Greeks look upon as shameful. For instance, what Roman would hesitate to take his wife to a dinner party? What matron does not frequent the front rooms of her dwelling and show herself in public? But it is very different in Greece; for there a woman is not admitted to a dinner party, unless relatives only are present, and she keeps to the more retired part of the house called "the women's apartment."

It is appropriate to take this passage as a starting point for a discussion of the Roman family, since the cohesive power of the family and its effectiveness as a social and moral force in the community must depend upon the degree of balance of its parts, that is to say, upon the relative position of the woman in the group. If, as in the Greek society of the fifth century, the wife and mother is practically ignored by society and the state, then the family atomizes, race suicide or a dangerous race-mixture involving inferior descent and neglect of children results, and even literature narrows into a partial expression of human emotions. If, on the other hand, a matriarchy arises out of an unwholesome promiscuity, the effectiveness of society is quickly endangered through the loss of directing control on the part of those who possess the greater physical force and continuity of energy.

It is curious that at Rome there were two opposing factors that early played a large part in determining the constitution of the family, one the juristic recognition of firm patriarchal rule, which in some respects tended to destroy the balance of the family, the other the equally firm social recognition accorded the matron, which tended to keep the balance unimpaired. To explain these facts historically seems to be impossible, and various attempts to approach the question from comparative sociology and anthropology have led to no better results. After the appearance of the first edition of Westermarck's *History of Human Marriage*, nearly forty years ago, there was a vigorous rivalry among scholars to unearth the survivals in Latin literature of exogamy and endogamy, of any and all the forms of matriarchy, marriage by capture, and totemism, but with no satisfactory conclusions. Comparisons with Berbers and Bushmen, Iroquois and Fuegians, soon broke down. The staid Roman family with its firm recognition of monogamy and father-rule goes back to the beginnings of history and beyond — probably far beyond. We are reaching the conclusion that cultural institutions are older in some parts of the world than we supposed, that somehow the ancestors of the Romans had done much thinking and organizing far back in unrecorded time, in such a way that their customs seldom fit into the elaborate sub-cultural schemes that anthropologists have too optimistically based upon a study of retarded or decadent races of the South Seas. Since we now recognize the fact that stable forms of marriage existed even among pre-anthropoid animals it would seem to be time to abandon the schematized hierarchy of marital institutions as in any way applicable to the anthropology of the more advanced races of historical time.

We may, however, legitimately discuss the question of how governmental forms and social groupings affected family institutions in historical times at Rome, for we leave much unexplained when we merely point out that in early Rome respect for the matron was high and remained so throughout the Republic. It is not so simple a question. The history of Greek society gives proof that within a period of a thousand years the family may pass through a series of the greatest changes while certain social traditions may remain static. In the days of Mycenean kingships, of which we have some plausible reflections in Homer and the great cyclical myths (for it seems now that the Mycenean princes were Hellenes), women like Andromache and Clytemestra held positions of as high respect as the courtly ladies of medieval France. Whether this was due to old Hellenic custom or to the consequences of regal institutions we cannot say. Centuries later when not only royalty but aristocracy as well had given way to democracy this well-balanced family of the heroic age had quite vanished. The old myths which to some extent portrayed the heroic life were somewhat refurbished for the stage, but in the Greek tragedies the spirit of courtly romance was but a pale ghost of the ancient reality. Aeschylus and Euripides lived in an age when it required a vigorous exertion of the imagination to re-people the old palaces with the princesses that even Homer had half forgotten.

The men who counted in public life in the age of Pericles seldom bore names of long standing. They were busy men of the new generation who had never known courtly manners, but had carried with them into high places the customs of the lowly and subdued Aegean population of Greece. The manners of the basement had moved up to the first floor; the Greek matron now lived silently and unobserved in the spinning room, and Romance had withered away.

Then, gradually, in the third century we note a change in Greek poetry, particularly in the poetry of the royal capitals outside of Greece built up by the despots that inherited the vast kingdom of Alexander. The royal families of these various courts — at Alexandria, Antioch, Pergamum, and elsewhere — gathered about them the usual troupe of courtiers, military men, administrative officials, poets to sing their deeds and lend distinction to their gatherings, and flatterers to keep them in good cheer. One peculiar circumstance contributes much to the promoting of feminine dignity in these new courts. The kings assumed the theory of Oriental despotism which ascribed divinity to kings, and, if the king was superhuman or divine, his children naturally were, daughters as well as sons. And a woman of divine origin and divine attributes is, of course, a candidate for thrones. That seems to be the reason why women have ascended thrones and high seats of power in despotic kingdoms so much more easily than in constitutional monarchies or republics. It may be a paradox that in the past women have profited more from autocracy than from democracy, but history says that it is so.

Naturally in these courts, where the wives, sisters, and daughters of kings became powerful by reason of birth, the poets, like Callimachus and Apollonius, dedicated verses to them, poems well packed with praise and flattery. These Alexandrian poets went even further: they rediscovered, through what they saw, the romantic element in the old myths which the classical dramatists had toned down into ethical didacticism. They became interested in the women of the heroic age, Medea, Hypsipyle, Oenone, Io, and the like, and dwelt now upon their human emotions and resulting tragedies. Many of the old stories were retold not as lessons of fate thwarting royal ambitions but rather as tales of frustrated passion. This new literature had some effect on life. Soon the customs of the courtly groups were aped by the dignitaries of the Hellenistic world, and to some extent the position of women was here and there altered, even in the life of the commons. But it is also clear that there is something rather artificial and hollow in the romance of Hellenistic poetry that found its inspiration in this new and transient courtly life. It did not last long enough to become permanent in the Greek world, and it was too circumscribed and exotic to take root in the decaying Greece of the mainland.

Now it is customary to see in the literature of Rome, in Catullus, Vergil, and the elegiac poets, a direct continuation of this new Hellenistic romance that sprang out of the courtly life of Alexandria. Yet the observation is true only in part. Catullus' brief epic is Alexandrian in spirit, and the elegiac poets do reflect in some measure the glamorous radiance of Alexandrian epigram; but it is a complete misunderstanding of the influence of Roman life upon literature to trace the basic conceptions of Vergil's great epic back to the Hellenistic court poetry. That poetry did, to be sure, portray powerful women who might suggest a model for Vergil's Dido, — though Vergil need not have gone so far afield for a model, — but the whole spirit of Vergil's romance is as far from Callimachus and Apollonius as Shakespeare is from Racine. To illustrate: Apollonius still was satisfied to employ the inadequate device of Cupid or the momentary glance to explain love — a business that he disposes of impatiently in a dozen lines:

But Eros the while through the mist-grey air passed all unseen. . . .
In the forecourt beneath the lintel swiftly his bow did he string:

From his quiver took he a shaft sigh-laden, unshot before:
With swift feet all unmarked hath he passed the threshold o'er,
Keen-glancing around: he hath glided close by Aison's son:
He hath grasped the string in the midst, and the arrow-notch laid
    thereon.
Straightway he strained it with both hands sundered wide apart,
And he shot at Medea; and speechless amazement filled her heart.
And the god himself from the high-roofed hall forth-flashing
    returned
Laughing aloud. Deep down in the maiden's bosom burned
His arrow like unto flame; and at Aison's son she cast
Side-glances of love evermore; and panted hard and fast
'Neath its burden the heart in her breast, nor did any remem-
    brance remain
Of aught beside, but her soul was melted with rapturous pain.

Vergil, who had lived in a wholly different atmos-
phere, comprehends the necessity of analyzing all the
psychological and emotional experiences involved —
the very types of experience that a reader expects to
find in a modern novel. Vergil felt that Aeneas must
learn the whole story of Dido's life of suffering before
he meets her, and Dido in turn must be acquainted
with the story of Troy. Aeneas is made to see the
version of his experiences that Dido has had carved
upon the doors of her temple, and then to behold the
queen as she is engaged in her work of building, of
giving commands to her people and of dispensing
judgements from her throne. Only then does Vergil
bring Aeneas and Dido face to face, and in a dialogue
packed with meaning let them learn to know each
other. Then in a night's banquet Aeneas is made to
tell the long story of his deeds in Troy and the seven
years of wandering. Now, at last, he feels that the
reader is ready for the tragedy of the fourth book.

Such careful preparation had not been given in the artificial romances of the Hellenistic age, because Hellenistic society had not created a life that made it essential. Those four books of the Aeneid mark an epoch in literature. We still celebrate Vergilian centenaries because it was Vergil who first conceived of a romance in a modern way, but not even he would have seen the necessity of it had he lived east of the Adriatic. It was the fact that he had been a child in a Roman family, had been nurtured by a Roman mother in a Roman home, that compelled him to write the story as he did. Such is the significance of the Roman family to any one who attempts to comprehend Roman literature.

The accounts of the Roman family in our handbooks on "Roman Life" need revising at several points. They are incorrect for various reasons. They are too largely based upon a literal interpretation of certain passages of the Roman law books. But laws seldom give an accurate reflection of social thinking at any one point. In my state it happens to be illegal to buy things on Sunday except for purposes of devotion or health. The law is two hundred years old, and in some respects became a dead letter long ago. We have hundreds of such ordinances upon our statute books, because our legislature has not taken the time to revoke them. In point of fact we do buy various articles on Sunday, even such mundane things as Mencken's magazine. Some day the proverbial New Zealander may write a dissertation to prove that Mencken's magazine was a health journal or a Sunday-school tract. Revocation of past legislation was even more difficult at Rome than with us, because the whole assembly had to be called together for a vote. Very few laws were ever annulled. They remained on the books, but were ignored by court and people when they were felt to be obsolete. Our historians have taken the written phrases of such laws too seriously.

Then again our interpreters have usually been rather old-fashioned scholars who have not been very prone to suspect the validity of Roman blue-laws. They disregard passages in Cicero's letters that reveal what are the actual practices of daily life and adhere to their belief in legal phraseology that seems more puritanic. They still quote a legal phrase that requires seven witnesses for a divorce when in point of fact a correspondent of Cicero happens to reveal in a casual letter to his friend how very informally the whole thing might be done. He writes thus: "Valeria Paula sent a letter of divorce to her husband without explanation the day he was to come home from his province: she is about to marry Decimus Brutus." The legal paragraph obviously does not agree with the customs in vogue, but the legalists have till very recently stuck by the law books and disregarded the facts.[1]

There are many such misunderstandings. Out of respect for what was considered substantive law the Romans never revoked the clause of the Twelve Tables which recognized the husband's complete control over his family. Even the clause which gave him, as formerly to the king, a judge's right of life and

death, was not revoked, though we know of no instance of its application to the matron. This was taken so seriously by a feminist who recently wrote a book on the status of women "through the ages" that she said: "The Roman husband did not divorce an unfaithful wife, he killed her." I might cite the law of Maryland, which till recently accorded the widow a very meager dower-right. The result was that in our state husbands adopted the practice of deeding over much of their property to their wives. When the laws move tardily, social custom may move all the faster. To an unusual extent women own the valuable property in this state. This will illustrate what I mean by saying that for a knowledge of Roman conditions we must be wary of taking conservative law books seriously where their phraseology does not conform to social practices.

The patriarchal family was one of the distinctive social institutions of old Rome. At the beginning of the Republic, 500 years before our era, the city had no machinery for the discovery and prosecution of crime. The pater familias was therefore, by custom, ruler and judge over this household, and his judgements (usually reached and pronounced after deliberation with several elders) were unlimited. Theoretically he could pronounce the death penalty upon any member of his family. We have in fact two well-authenticated instances of the death penalty pronounced against a son because of treason or military disobedience. This power of the father, recognized by the Twelve Tables, was not struck off the law books till imperial times, although custom limited its application year by year until it was practically emptied of meaning before it was revoked.

Now the institution is so striking that its purport and scope are readily overestimated. It is not necessarily a mark of a very primitive stage of culture, nor does it indicate an inevitable stage through which we may assume that many peoples have moved. The patriarchal system is often, as at Rome, linked with "self-help." It seems to arise spontaneously — as a modified form of it has arisen in the mountain districts of Kentucky — when migrant folk move away from their well-organized communities into dissevering hilly or forest country not yet placed under a central government. In such places unified legal control breaks up into fragments and may for a time disaggregate and fall upon the shoulders of the elders of small groups, or of the separate fathers of families where the groups are so small as to be only families.

The patriarchal system is in fact usually found in agrarian settlements, and often serves as a temporary makeshift between one strong government out of which families have migrated and the other that will be established as soon as the migrant groups have coalesced in their new home. Authority must rest somewhere, and a very natural seat of authority in such cases is the father. The existence of the patriarchal system does not necessarily imply that the matron, the sons, and the daughters are made to forfeit the love and devotion that family relations generally bring. Nor does it imply that the man is considered mentally superior to the woman. The very Twelve Tables that give us the first view of this system also reveal the strikingly modern custom of dividing intestate inheritances equally between sons and daughters. There could be no better proof of the essential equality of males and females than that, for it is a custom that has only recently been fully accepted by English law and is still unknown in some European countries 2500 years after we first find it at Rome. We may conclude, therefore, that the patriarchal system at Rome was purely a governmental accident — which probably arose in some period of migration from central Europe — and that it has no implications derogatory to any of the other members of the family.

Of course, when once well established, this system developed logical consequences of far-reaching effect. The father might live to hoary old age and have under his régime grandchildren and great-grandchildren all of whom would remain minors in respect to the parental property. Thus a son might theoretically reach the age of fifty years and attain to the highest offices of state — become, in fact, the chief magistrate of his state — and yet be a minor in the eyes of his father and be compelled to receive his financial support from his father. But he would not thereby be deprived of his deserts as a citizen. If the son were a magistrate, he might be in a position which would require that his father rise and stand in deference before his insignia of office, while theoretically his father would still have the power to condemn the son to death for any capital crime. Such was the early theory, but the hypothetical instance just cited shows that the patriarchal power was not allowed to interfere with civil requirements when the state acquired an efficient centralized government.

In the same way the patriarchal system logically required that the matron remain a minor with respect to property, either in the *manus* of her husband or of her father or guardian — for there were two common forms of marriage: of *manus*, in which case her husband became legally her guardian, and free marriage without *manus*, in which case her property did not depart to the husband's legal control. It is probable that the full effects of the former system did not reach into the classical period, for though we have a few instances in early history in which the bride assumed her husband's name, there are no sure instances after the Punic Wars. Thereafter she regularly retained her own family name. I do not mean to say that this fact implies that women no longer accepted the property-control of their husbands, but it does undoubtedly mean that such control was henceforth more a form than a reality. Readers of Cicero's letters know that the aristocratic ladies of classical times generally managed their own property or had financial agents who managed it for them. This must mean that on the signing of the marriage contract a woman did not surrender to her husband her legal rights, but remained a member of her father's family and received from her father the control of her share of family property. Here again we note a very wide early divergence between the phraseology of the law books that retained old legal formulae never revoked, and actual practice that made use of the right to disregard dead-letter laws and to invent legal expedients like fictive guardianships. As Cicero says in the pro Murena,[2] the lawyers invented a form of tutelage that could be placed at the disposal of the women themselves.

In Cicero's day, even though old laws had not been cancelled or changed, and even though the old institution of *patria potestas* was still recognized by statute, the Roman family was in some respects a freer association than the civilized world outside of Rome has since known. There usually was a marriage contract but it was not necessary. The mere verbal agreement of the two concerned, followed by familial union, was a legitimate marriage, and had been customary for at least four centuries. To such an extent did law protect this freedom from formality that a contract not to divorce was in classic law invalid.

To be sure, a formal contract of marriage with a formal ceremony was more usual. In such a case a contract between the parents of the two concerned, involving the consent of the man and woman, was usual, for a property settlement was quite the regular custom. But such a contract was not held enforceable in law. Furthermore neither state nor church was concerned in the affair, except that in cases of inheritance or legitimacy the court might later be called upon to inspect the evidence regarding the regularity of the marriage. Marriage, in a word, was in most cases a personal agreement. How marriages actually occurred we learn from a letter of Cicero, written when he suddenly heard from home that his daughter had become engaged to Dolabella, whom he heartily disliked, instead of to the very excellent Tiberius Nero, whom he favored. He writes to his best friend: "I assure you I hadn't expected that, for I had sent trusty messengers to my wife and daughter about the suit of Tiberius Nero, who had pleaded for my support. But they arrived in Rome after the betrothal was completed. I hope it will come out better than I fear it will; at any rate the women were quite taken by the gracious and polished manners of Dolabella. But I don't want to pick holes in him now." That is what *patria potestas* amounted to in Cicero's day. Not till the Empire did the state concern itself with marriage, and it was several centuries later that the church claimed a right to impress its sanction.

Hence divorce [3] was also a personal or at most a family matter during the Republic. From the earlier day, to be sure, we have very few instances of divorce, even as there are but few records of divorce in early New England. Puritanic life in a small community, where society insists upon conformity to strict family customs and where people of disheveled sentiments are made too uncomfortable to live in the community, could be relied upon to keep family life in order. But when Rome grew large and rich and spread over many neighboring cities, and when civil war broke out, that rent the old bonds between the powerful families of Rome so that the relatives of a man and his wife were thrown into opposing groups, then the contracts of parents and the mere verbal consent of the two concerned came, in many instances, to have but little force. In order to establish a divorce there was no need to go before a court or to satisfy the queries of a church. If the wife had charge of her own property she was at liberty to walk off with it if she chose. If her property was tied up with her husband's, an arbiter or a family council could decide upon a fair division of the property. There need in most cases be no court procedure. A letter of farewell, as in the case of Valeria Paula, cited above, or a personal message delivered by a friend sufficed in most cases to complete the divorce. There need be no cause offered and no explanation made either by the husband or the wife so far as the state was concerned.

One may well wonder what force in society was so powerful that it could counteract the tendencies of patriarchal custom and thus preserve for the woman this striking position of independence in the family, for she had an equality with the males in the Decemviral laws of inheritance, and in classical times, at least, the privilege of choice at marriage and divorce, and the right, so often used, of managing her own property. It seems to me that the secret lies largely in the permanence through many centuries of a dignified and powerful aristocracy. We have seen that in the Greek heroic age and again in the Hellenistic courtly period the emergence of powerful families where women as well as men were naturally of consequence evoked a romantic spirit that depended upon an equality of the sexes, whereas during the classical Greek period when democracy ruled, woman vanished into the gynaeceum.

One would hardly venture to hold that these parallels disclose the whole formula of Romance. In other places and at other times other factors have produced similar results. For instance, it may well be that in the period of the Troubadours it was not only courtly life and the enticing ladies of the many French palaces but also the influence of Christian doctrines of modesty together with a dash of Neoplatonism and a misreading of Ovid that entered into the effective recipe. Biology and climate may also shape a plausible formula. The frankly erotic poetry of southern climates contrasts very frequently with the more sentimental romance of northern lands, and the fact may perhaps find its explanation in the circumstance that in the south men reach a physical maturity before imaginative and emotional brooding produce the shimmer of poetry called romantic. There must be some such reason why the protecting cloisters of nunneries are so much more frequent south of the Alps than north. Or again, social exigencies may tell. In American frontier life, where men and women strode off into the plains to eke out a meager livelihood together in loneliness, they learned to respect and value each other as in few other places. The theories about the inferiority of women have found little favor in our western states.

The whole problem is an intricate one even for Rome, and the facts for Rome's early history are too far lost to afford an adequate explanation. But it is quite clear that there, as in certain epochs of Greece, the social customs that came into being in the houses of the great set the tone for the rest; and at Rome the noble families were numerous and through the Senate shaped an abiding régime.

Let us glance for a moment at the Roman villa-régime of the fourth and third centuries B.C., the epoch when the powerful nobles like Camillus, Fabricius, Publilius, Curius, the Aemilii, Hortensii, Cornelii, Fabii, Caecilii, Atilii, Marcelli, and a score of others maintained and expanded the power of Rome. Here was an agrarian-military nobility of about a hundred families that virtually administered affairs of state, held all the magistracies and judgeships, secured life membership in the Senate, controlled legislation and the legislative assemblies, conducted the wars, and directed the foreign policies of the state. These men were not very wealthy, and their homes had little silver plate and few works of art, and there were no courtly poets to sing flattering songs to them and their wives. Many of them, in fact, took their share in farm labor, as Ulysses did in the Greek heroic age. Their life, however, was one of dignity and significance. They had property enough in Campanian or Etruscan estates and in herds grazing on the hills of the Apennines to provide leisure for military duties and frequent attendance at the Senate. Influential in the council chamber and in the courts, they had many clients who called upon them in the morning hours for advice and aid and who with due deference attended them in their affairs of state. The business of a nation gave them importance and made them imperious and proud of their offices and rank. They treasured the annals of their ancestors through the generations, and their ambition was to leave a record of themselves that would be worthy of a place in the ancestral archives of which their children's children could be proud.

In these villas the right marriage was very important. The matron must be of good inheritance, of some political and social influence, and must bring a dowry of some value; for the children were expected to enter into the same life as their parents. And that required mental gifts, some leisure, and the combined influence of all the connections of both parents. It was also important — and for similar reasons — that parents find distinguished young men as husbands for their daughters. These young girls who were to be matrons in the great villas of the next generation were not sold for titles. Parental pride ensured that the marriage contract should not be such as to leave the child a prey to the whims of her husband. She could say yes or no, and her property was usually secured by her father to her keeping so that her position of independence and dignity would be guaranteed. Furthermore, since her husband would frequently be absent on campaigns or on state commissions and in court, it was important that at such times the decisions regarding the estate and the household should rest safely upon her shoulders. Her responsibilities in practical affairs and in the training of the children, which largely devolved upon her, and the importance of her own family connections were such that she was usually a member in family councils, even in such as concerned affairs of state.]

We have in Cicero's letters an interesting account of such a family council.[4] Mark Antony had just out-witted the faction of Brutus and Cassius at a meeting of the assembly, and it became necessary for the "liberators" to change their policy and reach a quick decision for the future. The men present at the council are Brutus, Cassius, and Cicero. The women are Porcia, the wife of Brutus, Servilia, his mother, and Tertia, the wife of Cassius. All partake in the discussion, but it is Servilia who gives the decisive plan and who promises through her personal influence to make it possible. There is nothing unusual in this council. The same kind of thing must have occurred frequently during the centuries when the aristocracy was in power.

The matron's position in the family was, of course, not a matter of a consistent evolution. The Twelve Tables, as we have seen, recognized equal division of intestate property among the children of both sexes, and also various forms of marriage, one of which left the matron free from her husband's authority. Two centuries later the sources seem to indicate a tempo-rary reversal of independence when the custom held, at least for a while, that the wife should assume her husband's name, and when also the law of inheritance intervened in favor of male heirs. The Voconian law, supported by Cato in 169 B.C., laid down the rule (not effective in case of intestacy) that a woman could not be the principal heir of a large estate. The purpose of this measure was to secure a considerable portion of senatorial estates for the young men who had to assume the burdens of administration and needed leisure for their public offices, which were, of course, not remunerative. In fact, it is in Cato's day that one hears not a little objection to the independence of the women, and it must be remembered, too, that it is in Cato's day that the Romans became acquainted with Greek households where women were closely restricted in freedom.

But by the end of the Republic the effects of the restrictive legislation of the Catonian period had been virtually annulled. Women no longer assumed their husband's name, the Voconian law had been weakened, partly by legal fictions, partly by new legislation; the force of the husband's *manus* had been attenuated even in cases (now rare) where strict forms of marriage had been used. In classical law the contract of marriage is virtually always the business of bride and groom and consists in the simple interchange of the questions between groom and bride: Visne mihi mater familias esse? Visne mihi pater familias esse? and, as we have said before, divorce depends now only upon a simple spoken or written declaration on the part of either party.

In the early days the burden of family duties was heavy in that education and moral training fell largely on the parents. There was no church with weekly sermons to help inculcate moral ideas. Example and precept dispensed by mother and father with a liberal use of family traditions handed down from illustrious ancestors had to serve where religion failed. When the matron led her children from one family portrait to another and recited the stories of valorous deeds that had earned each the high offices recorded below the statue, the children might silently infer what was expected of them. *Gloria* and *noblesse oblige* were powerful concepts in Rome's moral training.

Likewise in the general education of the children the parents took their duties seriously. We are told how Cato wrote out a child's history of Rome for his son [5] and how he took the boy out of doors and gave him lessons in manly sports, how Aemilius Paulus would supervise the studies and exercises of his children, and how Cicero chose to teach his son and nephew rather than trust them to tutors. Mothers also had an important share in this training. A large part of the credit for the successful education of the Gracchi, of Julius Caesar, and of Augustus is attributed by Tacitus to their mothers. Tutors and private schools were much in use, of course, but Roman parents remained close to their children. It is characteristic that when Cicero became governor of a province in Asia he took with him his son, Marcus, then fourteen years old, to see something of the world and its ways, and that later when Marcus, then about twenty, was studying at Athens, Cicero kept up a constant correspondence with his professors in order to keep well informed of his son's progress. The standard Roman definition of marriage — Nuptiae sunt conjunctio maris et feminae et consortium omnis vitae, divini et humani communicatio — proved its worth in the education of the children as in all else.

We should be quite in error if we supposed that because the father long retained an unusual degree of control over his children filial and parental affection were absent. Nowhere in pagan literature does one find such sentiments expressed so effectively as in Latin poetry. Vergil's national epic, which best reflects Roman ideals and manners, centers its most telling battle scenes about the tragedies of his very youthful heroes. Euryalus is pictured as only about sixteen years of age, but great-hearted and impetuously courageous. He goes to battle secretly with his friend, hoping to spare his mother many hours of apprehension for his safety. The mother's lamentation over her fallen son is one of the most intense passages in literature. The death-scene of the youthful Pallas, the requiem of Aeneas over his bier, the dirge of his father Evander, are filled with the same poignancy. And no reader of Vergil can forget how the boy Lausus rushes in to take the ax-stroke meant for his father, and how Aeneas honors this youthful enemy in death. The deep love of parents for children and of children for parents is not again conveyed so tenderly and convincingly till we reach Tennyson and Dickens. We utterly forget in reading these passages in Vergil that we are reading pagan poetry, and, needless to say, they are too Christian in spirit to suit the mood of our sophisticated postwar decade.

Augustus was the first to inject the idea of state

interference into the institution of marriage. Because of the protracted civil wars a disastrous pessimism regarding the future of society had led to an increasing avoidance of marriage and a marked decrease in the birth-rate. He therefore, without interfering in marital formalities or in the structure of the family, carried through legislation that was intended to increase the number of marriages and raise the birth-rate.[6] The proposals were of the same nature as those that have been adopted in France and Italy in consequence of the late disastrous war, and were confined chiefly to civil rewards and disabilities that were not compulsory. The freedom of divorce was not curtailed, in fact was not interfered with till several centuries later when the church was powerful enough to impose restrictions through canon law borrowed from the Orient.

The legislation of Augustus proved rather ineffectual and had to be modified by frequent grants of personal dispensation. But it did emphasize the important point of view that the state had a legitimate concern in the well-being of a social institution so important as the family, and it may have had a salutary influence by directing social thought to the question. There can be no doubt that through the next two centuries there was less whimsical divorce than had been usual at the end of the Republic. But it is also a plausible conjecture that this was due less to legislation than to a cessation of civil wars and to an increase of general social optimism owing to a return of peace and prosperity under the imperial rule. In fact the reforms of Augustus came at the very time when the need for them was about to become less urgent than before.

The Roman family is also interesting as providing the first instance we have in history of urbane society in the modern sense. In the Hellenistic courts there had been gay and cultured gatherings of men and women who met as equals and discussed serious matters or made small talk over their dinners. But the groups were very small, confined to very restricted court circles and always under the shadow of the imperial eyebrows. This society was not open to the people of the capital, nor did the customs of the court ever penetrate very far into urban life. At Rome, however, during the two later centuries of the Republic the situation was different. Here there were at least three hundred senators with their wives and family connections, making a social group of at least a thousand people of respected station, some leisure, some wealth, and in general of common interests. In the second century B.C. there was also, besides the senatorial class, an increasingly large group of knights — a kind of semi-nobility — many of whom were on friendly terms with the senators. In this social group large dinner parties were of such frequent occurrence and given on such a generous scale that the Catonian puritans felt compelled time and again to propose sumptuary laws to restrict them. (It was Cato, by the way, who created the perennial platitude: "We rule the world, but our women rule us.") Perhaps women were not as frequent participants at such gatherings as in modern society, but there are enough casual references to mixed gatherings at dinners, at theaters, and at festivals to prove that Roman social affairs were wholly different from anything that the world had known before.

It is characteristic that the early Roman dramatists when paraphrasing Menandrian comedy had their greatest difficulty in managing the feminine rôles. The plots of Greek comedy, of course, could not include women of the citizen groups because these did not appear out of doors. Hence they gave feminine rôles quite regularly to hetaerae. For Plautus [7] this created a dilemma: hetaerae as a class did not exist at Rome, and on the other hand Roman free-born women in the rather disheveled rôles of comedy would offend any Roman audience. He therefore did not attempt to translate Greek into Roman characters but kept the Greek setting and rôles intact. A little later the comic writer Titinius found a better solution. In adapting Greek plots for his togatae he recast them freely, abandoned the Greek setting with its constant use of the irregular love story, and, respecting the dignity of Rome's own august society, staged his love comedies in the small suburban towns where he could find the normal Roman equality of the sexes, free social relations, and also comic situations among folk that were not too staid to be represented on the boards. His plays seem to have been the first realistic comedies that portrayed types and romantic intrigues which we should recognize as quite modern.

These women of the early togatae were not exactly copies of the fashionable Roman matrons, — they were too simple and natural to be that, — but they owed some of their independence to the fashion set by the society of the villas. If we had the casual literature of the second century, now all lost, we should doubtless be able to reconstruct very modern-looking portraits of the grand-dame at the time of her greatest power. As it is, we must depend upon incidental references to her in later writers. Polybius happens to mention the position of Aemilia after her husband, the great Scipio, had died: "This lady," he says, "having participated in the fortunes of Scipio when he was at the height of his prosperity, used to display great magnificence whenever she took part in the religious ceremonies. For apart from the richness of her own dress and of the decoration of her carriage, all the baskets, cups, and other utensils of the sacrifice were of gold or of silver and were borne in her train on such solemn occasions, while the number of maids and servants in attendance was correspondingly large." The pageant of a passing consul could hardly have been of greater splendor. Regarding her daughter, Cornelia, the mother of the Gracchi, Plutarch chances to drop a few phrases that reveal a *salon* of a very modern type: "She had many friends and kept a good table that she might show hospitality, for she always had Greeks and other literary men about her, and all the reigning kings interchanged gifts with her." Indeed, Ptolemy VIII of Alexandria sued for her hand and offered her the crown of Egypt.

Cornelia is in fact a type of the influential women of
that day. Her husband, who spent most of his life in
administrative work and in travelling from Spain to
Syria, engaged in directing the foreign affairs of a
confused world, left the care and education of their
children to her. Since she was a woman of wide sympathies and extensive reading, she not only discussed
politics and philosophy with her children but she
secured the foremost Stoic philosopher of the day to
tutor her boys. Doubtless it was her influence and
the precepts of the tutors she chose that inspired her
two sons to undertake the reform of the Roman government. Later, indeed, she remonstrated with them
for carrying their proposals to the point of endanger-
ing the state and risking their own lives, but her
granddaughter, Sempronia, followed in the footsteps
of her sons.[8] It was she who opened her house to the
secret meetings of Catiline and his fellow-revolution-
ists, and her son in turn — Decimus Brutus — became one of the leading conspirators against the
tyrant Caesar and fought the triumvirs till he lost his
life in the contest. These two women were among the
greatest political forces in the last century of the
Roman Republic. Indeed, women of character and
influence stood by the side of a score of the statesmen
of the Ciceronian period and took their part in determining policies of state. To prove it we have but
to mention such names still well known as Porcia,
Aurelia, Clodia, Calpurnia, Mucia, Servilia, Julia,
Cornelia, Sempronia, Tertia, Junia, Terentia, Hor-
tensia, Sulpicia, and Fulvia. If we count the Roman

names in the Classical Encyclopaedia, we shall find a relatively longer list of women than in any nation's record before the nineteenth century.

In the late Republic the observer may find symptoms of aristocratic family conceptions that are not very wholesome in their consequences. In a society of political nobility powerful influences may be conveyed from family to family by marriage, and what we may call "dynastic" unions may result in which a woman, simply because of her position or influence, may be asked to sacrifice herself for the furtherance of political ends. Caesar's marriage to a consul's daughter, Pompey's union with Julia, the daughter of Caesar, Octavian's marriage with Scribonia and later with Livia, his sister's prearranged union with the unfaithful Mark Antony, would, of course, have had no value in a society where women counted for nothing. Julia, Octavia, and Livia were expected to bring character, dignity, and influence with them, and they did. But it was, of course, the civil disturbances of the day that had suggested the advisability of such dynastic marriages, and it was in a measure the betrayal of woman's authority to ask her thus to serve a political purpose. Needless to say such marriages were often unhappy. Octavia bore her sorrows in silence when betrayed by Antony, but Augustus' own daughter when compelled to marry Tiberius for reasons of state refused to surrender a Roman woman's customary right to form her own attachments. Women had not been trained in the kind of submission that such politics seemed to demand, and Julia's recalcitrance led to disaster. Indeed, the story of the Julian dynasty contains a list of many powerful and headstrong women who rebelled disastrously against the new demands for sacrifice on the part of the throne.

There is another aspect of these marriages that may be of interest in literary history. We are accustomed to say that Ovid's poetry was influential in shaping the theory of courtly love in the early days of the medieval French lyric. This we may grant in some small measure, though it might be more correct to say that the men and women of the medieval French courts had passed through experiences which made it possible for them to appreciate Ovid's peculiar view of men and women. Again in the seventeenth century, when French poets like Scarron began to write satires on froward women who were supposed to be skilled in the art of coquetry, we hear again of the influence of the Augustan poets. Since the last great war our novelists have once more recurred to the old theme in every possible kind of contra-romance, and women novelists, skilled in self-revelation, have led the way. This time we know better than to blame Ovid, for in England and America where the phenomenon is most patent we can diagnose our own social behavior. After all, human behavior gives the cue to the essayist and novelist. Literary influence is often merely an afterthought. A teacher of schoolgirls recently remarked that whereas twenty years ago her pupils used to call Aeneas a cad, now they lose their patience with

Dido. There is a volume of social history behind that fact.

There is some significance in the fact that critics have referred to Augustan poets to explain certain later manifestations of feminine assertiveness. It is doubtless because Augustan life for the first time evolved these peculiar social conditions that poets undertook to write about women as Ovid did. Ovid was after all, as he admits, an echo of what he heard. Society had in his day merely progressed in the direction that the famous Clodia had indicated two decades before. Clodia was a woman with five centuries of proud aristocracy behind her. Reduced to financial straits by political misfortunes, she had married a rather dull plebeian, Metellus, who had some means and political connections. She was beautiful, witty, and far more intelligent than her husband. In politics she saw more clearly than he. When Metellus was absent from Rome on foreign campaigns and state commissions, she was not only the manager of the household and the estate, but she looked after his political interests. At her *salon* gathered the more brilliant men of Rome, and it was she who made out the list of visitors. What that finally led to we know from the passionate verses of Catullus. Considering the times, considering the ambitions and social liberty of such women, the reader is quite prepared for such a dénouement. Let this situation continue through two or three decades of civil strife during which the leading families found it even more necessary to consolidate political influences by means of shrewd family unions and we have the society of Ovid. Women of station and pride gave their consent to political marriages, with reservation as to their own property and no less as to their human desires, because political alignments might shift at any moment. Such marriages were seldom happy, and there was no religious sacrament or state contract, no *potestas* or *manus*, to hold the two together longer than some temporary advantage dictated. In such conditions, if a woman was human she was apt to discover before long that there were more desirable men than the one allotted to her, and seeing one she might make some effort to attract his attention. It was Ovid's discovery that his society was based on equal rights and privileges and that the old social restraints were no more, and he enjoyed describing the resulting complications. He did not teach society a lesson, he described what he saw.

Such were the social conditions of Ovid's day after the free marital unions of Rome had fallen under the wrecking processes of the civil wars. The dangerous consequences were not the result of old Roman custom. For five centuries or more free marriages, that is without *manus*, without church or state bonds, had existed with as complete satisfaction as the history of the institution has known. What is surprising to the modern who is accustomed to a church and state supervision of the family is that the Roman family prospered for several centuries with no supervision but that of social opinion.

SOCIAL FACTORS IN RELIGIOUS CHANGES

DURING the Roman Republic the state had charge of religious cults, decided which gods might have temples or shrines within the city walls, built the temples or extended to individuals the permission to build them, appointed the priests, and paid the expenses of the accepted cults. The state recognized the necessity of religious worship but seemed always to fear that it might assume dangerous aspects unless carefully supervised. As a result worship was orderly, dignified, and in many instances beautiful, but for centuries it was rather impersonal, cold, and ritualistic, and, as in Greece, it had hardly any connection with ethical teaching. This was its nature even before Greek rationalism and skepticism came in. The Romans themselves, before they came into contact with outsiders, seem to have had a strong aversion for demonstrative religious rites.[1]

During the early Empire, however, a very remarkable change is to be noticed. By A.D. two hundred the eastern cults of Mithras, Isis, and a dozen Baals of Asia were found all over the West. One might then see on the streets of Rome gorgeous processions of devotees celebrating exotic rites in extravagant songs and dances. Men talked everywhere about purification from sin, immortality, the immanence of god in the soul, and salvation by ablution in blood. These new cults usually throve upon private support without asking for state aid. What had brought about the great change? Can it be that these devotees were the descendants of the unemotional Romans who in Scipio's day were satisfied with the stately ritual of the pontiff? Or are these Romans a different people? This is one of the perplexing questions of history and many attempts have been made to answer it. The question is a part of the very large problem of how religions spread. There are, of course, many ways. The spread of the Moslem religion was usually by way of conquest. The Christian religion has generally been carried by oral propaganda, but sometimes also by folk movements. It is well known that in America the Catholic church has grown not so much by preachment as by the diffusion of the immigrant Irish, Italians, Austrians, Poles, and other peoples who were members of the church at home. The Jewish synagogues in America now claim over four million members, but very few of them are converts from other religions. The devotees of Confucianism and Buddhism (except for a few pathological exhibits) are immigrants, not converts. Those who have studied the history of aberrant religions in America would hardly be inclined to assert that the success of cults always varies directly with their moral worth.

Now the strange thing about the success of the Oriental mystery religions at Rome is that their devotees did not preach or proselyte, nor did any of these religions claim to be the only way to salvation. Yet they spread with very great rapidity through the western world. Cumont, our foremost authority on the religions of the Roman times, still holds in the fourth edition of his book on Oriental religions, as he did in his first edition, that a great religious conquest can be explained only by moral causes. He thinks, in fact, that these religions offered something of greater moral value and something of stronger human appeal than the old Roman religion had and that they accordingly were consciously adopted as superior religions. Toutain,[2] in writing of religion in the western provinces, expressed some doubt on this point by showing that in the West, at least, the devotees of the new religions were largely Oriental immigrants who merely retained their native practices and beliefs in their migrations. Dobschütz, who lectured in America before the war, approximated to Cumont's point of view. His belief was that the Roman state had for social reasons suppressed every manifestation of mysticism, which, however, burst forth later at the touch of Oriental religions because it satisfied a human need. In this way these new religions, he thought, prepared the Roman people for the coming of Christianity. His argument was very persuasively presented, but to those of us who had been working with the Roman inscriptions it seemed quite evident that what Toutain had found in the western provinces was in general true for the rest of the Roman world as well, namely that the success of the new cults was largely determined by the movements of peoples who already held to these cults. More recently Professor La Piana has developed this idea even with respect to Christianity, a subject that lies somewhat outside the scope of my present theme. In undertaking to give a brief review of the invasion of the mystery religions I may preface the sketch with the remark that Cumont has successfully shown that these religions had much persuasive value and that not a few Occidentals were in fact converted to them; but I still believe that their success in the western world was largely due to social causes, due indeed to the fact that the people of Rome were largely of immigrant stock in the day when the change in religion took place.

In a land where all men are assumed to be "born free and equal" it may seem invidious to speak of racial stocks. However, the question of our own folk-mixture need not enter into the discussion. Rome's "melting pot" was very different from ours, for here, after all, we admit only Europeans, who differ from us mainly in superficial cultural habits which are quickly modified in our public schools. Rome's experience was quite different. The early Romans had been a fairly homogeneous folk of puritanic habits and simple wants; they were liberty-loving, dreading nothing quite as much as autocratic rule and the possible loss of their independence. On the other hand the Asiatic immigrants who came to Rome had been brought in chiefly as slaves from regions where self-government had not been known for thousands of years. In Mesopotamia and Egypt, from which they had their religions, the kings had for ages been autocrats and owners of the land for the simple reason that the crops depended upon vast canal systems that only supreme autocrats could control. Thousands of years of autocracy imply thousands of years of abject submission, and this in turn naturally resulted in a stamping out of the more independent spirits and a propagation of the more submissive. Those who could not endure despotism would get out or be eliminated. Thus it was that in time much of western Asia and Egypt became the home of peoples whom the Romans looked upon as spineless and "born for slavery." Their religions were characteristically filled with magical formulae designed to "release" the worshipper. They had suffered from oppression, want, hunger, and every form of abuse and tyranny, and longed for a future life where there would be plenty to eat and no labor. They had drawn the conclusion, typical of the temperamentally meek and lowly, that they had somehow brought upon themselves the wrath of God and must find in religion the ablution from the sin or ritual taint which had caused the affliction, but in none of these religions does this sense of sin lead to the clean moral vision of a Hosea. The oppressed peoples longed for a savior or for some saving incantation, for initiations into the groups of elect who were guaranteed salvation; above all else they desired an eternal life of pleasure to compensate them for their earthly life of misery. In a word, the peculiarities of the mystery religions are not so much to be attributed to primitive survivals of nature-rites or to climatic conditions (though these also count) as to the

long experiences of these peoples in lands where despotism had been a necessity, or in lands so close to
these that they fell under the same régime.

On the contrary the Greeks and Romans, who had
lived in lands where individualism could thrive as it
could not in Mesopotamia and the Nile valley, developed faith in their own judgements and in their own
capacities. During the Republic this life was their
chief concern; they did not worry about any other.
What they wanted they were used to getting by their
own efforts, without resort to prayer or incantation.
It would seem that the age-long processes of survival
and selection under peculiar conditions had begot different races in Mesopotamia and in the Greco-Roman
peninsulas which determined their political behavior
and no less their religious temperaments.[3]

Now there is, of course, some plausibility in the old
hypothesis that in the late Republic the Romans "lost
their nerve" when they realized that their republican
forms of government did not suffice to govern the
empire they had created and when they fell into a
civil strife which necessitated the use of a strong centralized government. But the theory that this dis-
heartening experience alone accounts for their submission to autocracy and for their ready acceptance
of authoritarian mysticism in religion disregards too
facilely the decided temperamental peculiarities of
the Romans. The determining fact is that the old
Roman stock had by this time dwindled and largely
given way to Asiatic peoples who were of a different
fibre.

How this came about I have tried to tell elsewhere,[4] and it need not be repeated at length. We know that the old Italic stock suffered severely in all the wars when the legions were conscripted from property-owning citizens; we know also that emigration to the new provinces went on steadily, especially as slave-economy supplied cheap labor and tainted all industries so that poor citizens avoided them. We know how such slaves increased at Rome by breeding, and how slaves were brought in in large consignments, not only war captives from every region of the world, but also slaves of the trade that the dealers of the Aegean ports handled daily by the thousands. We also know how readily they gained their emancipation and with it Roman citizenship. After Cato's day the Roman citizen-census increased to a very considerable part through the immigration due to the slave trade and through subsequent emancipation of such slaves. In the days of Augustus it is probable that half the citizens of the capital were of non-Roman stock. A census of the names on the epitaphs near Rome has shown that in Hadrian's day less than fifteen per cent of those recorded reveal a pure Roman ancestry, and most of the other eighty-five per cent prove to be of eastern origin. This seems to me to be the prime factor in the decided spread of the Oriental cults in the West. In the main it means not that the Occidentals of the old type had been converted to the new religions — though a few had — but that the Asiatics had brought with them to the West the religions of their ancestors, the religions that suited their own temperaments. A partial parallel of some significance for the situation at Rome can be cited from the statistics of New York. In 1800 there were about five hundred Jews in New York City, now there are over a million; in 1800 there was one Roman Catholic congregation, now this church claims two million members in the city, only eight per cent of whom are converts. In 1920 only eighteen per cent of the population of New York City could claim American ancestry of two generations.

Now, before giving a hasty review of the westward invasion of the Oriental cults I would remark that during the Republic there was no religious persecution at Rome, although the state insisted upon its right to keep disliked shrines outside the city walls. Liberty of conscience was respected, and any form of worship was legal provided it did not involve immorality and provided it did not insist upon official recognition inside the city walls. Temples and shrines of all kinds of deities could freely find a place in the Campus Martius or other suburbs. Let me also add that the road from Mesopotamia to Rome was a long one and that few temptations from that source could reach Rome in the early days. It was not until Alexander the Great conquered the East that the routes of communication were first opened. Alexander has been praised endlessly for Hellenizing the East. It is not so frequently remembered that while he laid the cultural road from Greece to the Euphrates he thereby opened the gates of the West to the cultures of Mesopotamia. Much of the obscurantist credulity that settled over Europe in the late imperial times flowed in by that gate. When you see printed in your daily papers the preposterous "horoscope" of each day, when you notice that a textbook on "Astrology" written by an American woman has become a "best-seller," you may thank Alexander the Great and his ambition to marry East and West for these humiliating facts.

Only twice during the Republic do we hear of mystery religions attracting popular attention at Rome. In 204, during the Punic War, an oracle was found that seemed to advocate the importation of Cybele (Magna Mater) from Phrygia. She was the chief deity of the region whence the Romans claimed to have come. The Romans knew nothing about the cult, but they sent for the rude image and built a temple for her, and Phrygian priests were imported to perform her rites correctly, since initiation into her priesthood required an act of deviration to which no Roman citizen could legally submit. But the orgiastic rites with their unseemly dances, the din of cymbals, and the crude appeal to sex instincts did not please the Romans, and for over 200 years the rites, though they were continued at state expense, were confined inside the walls of the Palatine precinct. All this time we do not hear of any Romans participating in the worship, though they looked with some amusement at the fantastic processions of the priests at the spring festival. The acceptance of Cybele was an accident, and for over two centuries had no influence upon Roman religion.

Twenty years later we learn that the mysteries of Dionysus (Bacchus) were performed by many people at Rome, that the senate, spurred on by Cato, investigated the nocturnal orgies of this cult, pronounced them immoral, and suppressed them with severity. It has usually been supposed that Egyptian priests or perhaps soldiers who had been converted while serving in Asia had introduced the Dionysiac mysteries to Rome and that this is the first instance of the spread of an Asiatic religion by propaganda. It is, however, very difficult to believe that Egyptians then had any influence at Rome or that Roman soldiers, living for a year in camp in Asia and incapable of comprehending more than a few words of Greek, should have been converted to a mystical cult in such numbers that two years after their return the religion could count thousands of devotees at Rome. The explanation [5] for the existence of the rites at Rome seems rather to be that the Greek captives of Tarentum and Locri, some 30,000 of whom had been brought to Rome twenty years before the date in question and many of whom had meanwhile gained freedom and citizenship, had carried their favorite rites with them. The question is of importance in the story of how foreign religions spread at Rome. In this case, as in so many other instances, the worshippers seem to have been captives who continued in their new home the worship of their native deities. We have no right to assume from Livy's account that native Romans had to any extent been converted.

It is also interesting to note the Senate's procedure

in the matter. Cato, a puritan and a strong national-
ist, was at this time opposing the expansionistic
politics of Scipio. His chief weapon of attack was to
proclaim that Roman morals were being endangered
by contact with Greek and Asiatic ideas and customs.
That he drove hard against the Dionysiac mysteries
is, therefore, not surprising. But it was not a faith or a
creed that he labored so hard to suppress; it was the
rites performed in suspicious nocturnal meetings that
were pronounced immoral and were accordingly pro-
scribed. The Senate indeed so far guarded itself from
offending the deity that it permitted the worship of
Dionysus provided not more than five persons participated at any one place and provided the worshippers took an oath before the praetor that they were
obliged to fulfill vows they had already made. It
should be noted that liberty of conscience was recognized, so far as the religious faith was concerned.
Thereafter we hear little of this cult at Rome.

During the last two centuries of the Republic, war
captives were brought in from every quarter of the
world and hordes of slaves were bought, especially in
the East. But scattered in the general confusion and
stunned by their misfortunes, many of the slaves temporarily lost touch with their own cults. It required
some time for nationalistic groups of freed slaves to
congregate in definite parts of the Roman foreign
quarters and to reëstablish old cults in such promi-
nence as to attract attention.

The Jews were among the first to form a distinctive
foreign group at Rome. They had begun to migrate

westward during the Seleucid-Maccabean wars and a colony of immigrants was known at Rome in the Gracchan period. To this a horde of captives brought by Pompey in 62 B.C. added a large number of freedmen — for the Jew was noted for the speed with which he won his freedom. A slave who had conscientious scruples against working every seventh day and against eating Roman food was not considered very profitable, and when his friends offered to pay for his freedom the offer was readily accepted.

In this group, the Romans apparently met for the first time citizens who were required by their religion to disobey Roman laws. If conscripted for the army, the police, or fire department, the orthodox believers generally refused to take the official oath of service, and they could not do their share of the required work on sabbath days. This must have aroused no little antagonism in Roman officialdom. Since we hear of no prosecutions for refusal to perform civil duties, it is likely that the Senate on Pompey's advice either legislated in favor of exemptions, as we know that Caesar did, or, in view of the small number involved, disregarded the objectors as harmless fanatics. According to documents quoted by Josephus provincial governors regularly excused Jews from state service that was not consistent with the Jewish creed. Rome did not like to incur the wrath of any divinity. Caesar very readily granted exemptions because he had been aided by a troop of Jewish auxiliaries when besieged at Alexandria in 47; in fact he seems to have owed his life to them. The precedent set by him in recognizing the claims of a foreign religion as paramount to Rome's political claims was important, and when the Jews established their right to set up synagogues and to observe their own rites at Rome, other groups probably felt encouraged to form their own religious communities there also. The Jewish religion, however, despite an active propaganda, can hardly be said to have gained many converts outside the racial group.

Worshippers of Isis, chiefly Egyptians and Alexandrians, were known at Rome before Caesar's day, coming chiefly, we may presume, in the train of Ptolemy Alexander in 81 and of Ptolemy Auletes in 57, but they were not numerous.[6] However, when in 45 B.C. Cleopatra, with a large part of her court and a numerous retinue of servants, came to Rome to live in Caesar's suburban villa, she seems to have asked for a temple of Isis. At any rate the Senate, in carrying out Caesar's promises after his death, ordered such a temple to be erected, though apparently it was never completed. The Isis cult contained many practices strange to old Romans, for it included elaborate secret initiations and rites of "purification" that were designed to secure the soul happiness in a future life.[7] However, there was no political objection to this religion, since the devotees of Isis were free to take any oath required by the state, and since the requirements of Isis in no way interfered with the duties devolving upon Roman citizens. Later, to be sure, the cult met with hostility on moral grounds, because after the departure of Cleopatra and her courtly retinue the worshippers that were left were chiefly dancing girls, courtezans, and the like, and these for a generation at least made the rites malodorous. For this reason Augustus took the occasion after the defeat of Antony and Cleopatra, when everything Egyptian fell into ill favor, to remove the shrines from inside the city walls, but the worship was not prohibited.

Foreign groups now grew rapidly and became conscious of their strength. Favored by Caligula, Claudius, and Nero, who depended heavily upon the aid of clever Alexandrian freedmen and Alexandrian officials in the library and fiscal offices, Isis worshippers reintroduced the cult openly and no further effort was made to disturb it.[8] During the Empire this religion had the unusual advantage of enjoying the support of Alexandrian merchants of good standing who had well-staffed offices in all the harbors and market places of the Roman world. It is interesting to find, however, that few native Occidentals accepted its rites. The remains of shrines and cult statues are found today where we know that Alexandrian traders had their docks, where soldiers from Egypt were stationed, where eastern traders resorted to the various camps, and where low-class Egyptian entertainers and slaves are known to have lived.[9] The cult was carried as far as its devotees went — and with but few exceptions, no farther. It never spread by conversion or proselyting except to a very limited extent through personal contacts among Greek-speaking slaves and among workmen engaged in commerce on the sea.

Claudius also opened the priesthood of the Cybele

worship to Romans,[10] it would seem, by permitting a fictional substitution for the rites of emasculation that old Roman law had forbidden. Perhaps some of his Phrygian freedmen were accountable for this favor to their goddess, but since it had been a vestal of the Claudian family who had brought the Cybele statue up the Tiber, the Claudian family had become the official patrons of the cult for two centuries, and we need not seek further for an explanation of the emperor's benevolence. However, even after this revision the number of Cybele worshippers at Rome remained small. Not until a century later do we find evidence in inscriptions that Romans of some station took part in the rite of gaining immortality by washing themselves in the blood of slain offerings. And these Romans are often of Phrygian descent. The cult of Magna Mater, though she had, by accident, early entered the pantheon, never spread far beyond the circle of those people whose ancestors had worshipped Cybele in Anatolia.

Mithraic worship spread over a larger area than the Egyptian and Phrygian religions. Mithraism was a revised version of an old Persian cult much contaminated with Chaldaic astrology, and was very popular in Mesopotamia and in all of inner Anatolia whence Rome drew many slaves and many cohorts of auxiliaries during the second and third centuries. We have the names of over twenty Oriental regiments of auxiliaries stationed in various parts of Europe, and we know that these regiments were regularly refilled by recruits from among their countrymen.[11] We also know that for several years Marcus Aurelius used large parts of five western legions in his Parthian wars and that these legions returned westward with eastern contingents. In the third and fourth centuries there were frequent shiftings of forces between the East and the West. The Mithraic shrines at the forts, canabae, and towns on and near the Rhine-Danube frontier can be adequately accounted for by the presence of such soldiers and their children. Here and there we find evidence of a few Occidental converts, but they are not numerous. Renan's oft-quoted statement that Mithraism spread so rapidly in the West that it might well have become the state religion instead of Christianity, no one now accepts.

This religion taught a plausible Persian dualism (both philosophical and ethical), promised immortality to its devotees, was promoted by organized congregations that provided all the advantages of fellowship, possessed an elaborate series of secret initiations, and promulgated a system of rules which took some cognizance of moral values. But it had no central organization to direct propaganda, no preachers to spread its creed, no standard book to give it authority or to define its orthodoxy, no sacred scriptures of essential stories, no claim to a monopoly in salvation, and the oral traditions concerning its founder were both childish and without significance. In short, it lacked almost every essential for becoming a universal religion.

A great many other cults also found welcome throughout the Empire as the Roman world became more and more a "melting pot" — for example, the cults of Baalbek, of Palmyra, of several Syrian Baals —Baals that, in the West, came to be identified with Jupiter. After carefully scrutinizing the inscriptions that record the names of their worshippers, we can only come to the conclusion that none of these Oriental types of worship gained any firm foothold among the native Occidentals. They followed their devotees over the world, but they made few converts in the West.

There are two apparent exceptions to this general statement. In the third century while Heliogabalus and his cousin Alexander were emperors at Rome, the Baal of Hemesa (Homs) in Syria received great honors from high officials everywhere. The reason for this fact has long been known. During his governorship in Syria Septimius Severus, a man of Punic or Numidian race, had married a Syrian woman — the daughter of the priest-king of Hemesa. After many vicissitudes their grandson, Heliogabalus, then a priest of the local Baal, was elevated to the throne of Rome by the army which had been devoted to Septimius. This new Syrian emperor naturally introduced his own Baal — under its Greek name, Heliogabal — to Rome and insisted that his be the recognized cult. Servile courtiers everywhere pretended to favor the worship and inscribed fulsome dedications to this god. That the cult won any general respect no one would hold. It disappeared as soon as the Afro-Syrian dynasty disappeared.

The other cult that had a similar history was that

of *Sol Invictus* which was foisted on Rome by Aurelian a generation later. This emperor had risen in the army from the lowest ranks. His mother seems to have been a priestess of a Sun or Baal temple on the borders of Dacia. There were then several colonies of Syrians in that province. In his army service Aurelian had met many worshippers of Mithras, the sun-god of Parthia, and in the East he had offered sacrifices to the Baal-sun-god of Palmyra as well as to the local Baal at Hemesa. When he reached the throne, he accordingly shaped a new sun-worship which seemed to him to be a reasonable syncretism of the cults which were so popular among a large part of his soldiers. He invited all the devotees of the various Syrian Baals, of Mithras, and even of the Roman Jupiter to recognize their respective gods in *Sol Invictus*. By merging several deities in one he was, of course, far more successful than Heliogabalus had been, and he also lived long enough to accustom the officials under his command to erecting a great many dedications to the new deity. The cult, therefore, did not die at once, and it is probable that our celebration of Christmas on the twenty-fifth of December is due to the endurance of the chief holiday of this successor of Mithras. But, again, the cult did not win the general favor of people throughout the Empire, and the numerous official dedications do not truly represent the status of the cult in public opinion. Already, while officialdom was performing these rites, Christianity had found masses of worshippers everywhere. And after the death of Diocletian, who tried in vain to revive the cult of *Sol Invictus*, it dwindled very rapidly, carrying Mithraism down with it.

The point that I have tried to underscore is that all these attractive mystery cults of the East, though they spread widely and at times numbered among their devotees hundreds of thousands, won few converts in the West. Most of their worshippers in the West were immigrants, natives of the lands in which these religions had arisen, and these foreigners made only occasional converts among their new friends at Rome.

The chief reason, I suppose, why scholars do not agree on the question as to whether or not these mystery cults gained proselytes in the West is that the inscriptions do not give us as explicit information about their devotees as we should like. It has been customary in past researches to class all citizens and all who bore the *tria nomina* as "Romans." This classification, however, will not suffice for our purposes.[12] Every slave received at manumission the coveted three names, praenomen, nomen, and cognomen. The last was supposed to be his previous servile designation, and a careful study of the standard servile names will accordingly reveal the fact that a great many of those who bear three names on the inscriptions are not of Roman stock, but are of slave or ex-slave extraction. However, we must penetrate further. In the second generation even those of servile stock had the right to slough off the betraying servile cognomen and assume a more respectable one. When they did so, their cognomina no longer revealed their provenience. However, their epitaphs often mention parents, or near relatives of servile origin, and thus betray their previous station. Again, we know that after the first century soldiers of most of the legions and of all the cohorts were recruited in the provinces, and that after Hadrian's day they were quite regularly non-citizens, at least up to the time of recruiting. Hence we may add these soldiers also to the lists of foreigners, even though they bear good Roman names. Lastly, certain posts, such as stewardships, were regularly held by slaves, and certain positions, such as the sevirate in the municipalities, and the procuratorships in the lower civil service, were as regularly held by ex-slaves. After all these indications have been noted it will often turn out that where one scholar has loosely reported only fifty per cent of the worshippers of some foreign deity as being foreign, the percentage will by accurate count rise to ninety, and might, indeed, rise still higher if we had all the evidence.

Too much has also been made of the fact that state, military, and municipal officials often dedicate gifts to some of these foreign deities. At a time when Rome was full of foreigners, sound political policy suggested the advisability of humoring these people by an open benevolence toward their favorite cults. We have all had enough experience with politicians and political speeches made to lodges, churches, immigrant groups, and alumni assemblies to know how to interpret such flattery. It reveals something of the influence of the group that is powerful enough to exact it, but not necessarily very much about the inclinations of the victim. In a word, the student who investigates the scattered evidence in this field must read with full knowledge and poised judgement, and it is only after an examination of much of the discriminating work of recent years that I have ventured to offer the conclusions outlined above.

In my brief statement of the spread of the Oriental cults, I have purposely omitted any reference to certain learned mysteries like the Orphic and Neo-Pythagorean creeds that for a while gained a hearing among the aristocracy of the late Republic and early Empire.[13] Our information about these mysteries and their place at Rome is very meager. We know that Roman nobles like Cicero, largely out of curiosity, gained admission to the Orphic initiations at Eleusis, and that at times, as in Cicero's *De Republica*, the experience provided phrases and ideas for a pretty excursus into eschatological myths, but the main body of Cicero's writings gives proof enough that mysticism had no real significance for him except in the one brief period of a few weeks when he searched every possible creed in his effort to find consolation after his daughter's death.[14] Orphism had no abiding influence at Rome. It left less of a mark at Rome than the least of the Oriental religions. Macchioro's fascinating book, called *From Orpheus to St. Paul*, is valuable chiefly for its discussion of this "religion" in Greek lands. It seems to me somewhat to overstate its significance at Rome.

The Neo-Pythagorean cult also has, perhaps, been overvalued in various recent books.[15] In the late Republic a certain Etruscan pedant, Nigidius Figulus, gained some fame by trying to convert his friends to the obsolete doctrines and dietary rules of Pythagoras with their later accretions of symbolism. He made little progress and was banished by Caesar, apparently for political reasons. The beautiful designs in stucco reliefs found in the so-called "Underground Basilica" a few years ago have recently been explained with some plausibility as symbolic representations of the beliefs of this group. If this could be proved, we should have to believe that a circle of rather important Romans held secret sessions in a Neo-Pythagorean "church" during the first century A.D. The question arises, however, whether these pictures and those of the Villa Farnesina, of the Villa Item, and of the "Homeric corridor" of Pompeii are consistent representations of cults for which these rooms and crypts served as "churches." This has not yet been proved. It may simply be that plasterers and frescoers from Alexandria had been hired to decorate these walls and took their charming designs from note-book sketches that they had made in Alexandria. They may possibly be no more significant of the beliefs and creeds of the owners than are the pictures of Greek deities and myths painted on the lunettes of our Congressional Library at Washington. Some day a thousand years from now I can well believe that archaeologists patching together the fragments of our decorated walls will attempt to prove that in the last decade of the nineteenth century our Congress deserted Christianity and reverted to the old faith in the Olympic deities.

That the diffusion of the Oriental cults prepared the way for the spread of Christianity in the West seems to me to be true only in the sense that the presence of those cults testifies to the diffusion of eastern peoples who were peculiarly prepared to receive the Christian teachings. It is not my intention to discuss the rapid spread of Christianity, except in so far as it connects with the question of the new populations of Rome. Christianity, in so far as it inherited the ideas and practices of the Jewish religion, which in turn had been somewhat affected by Mesopotamian ideas,[16] might, of course, be considered one of the Oriental religions. But it is so immensely superior to all of them in its ethical doctrine that it would be unscientific to place it in the same class. It has been a popular diversion among scholars to hunt for Mithraic and Orphic conceptions in the Gospels and in the letters of St. Paul.[17] There is no doubt that the early preachers of Christianity, like the successful preachers of any time, adopted current phraseology now and then in order to make their messages comprehensible. But the fact remains that after one has examined the confused ethics, the hedonistic materialism, and the crude symbolism of the mystery cults and then reads the Sermon on the Mount, one must admit that one has come into another world of religion. The Oriental cults worried much about "purification," but such purification was still at bottom a ritualistic cleansing that had little effect upon man's moral or social behavior; it merely provided a palliative, a way of escape. Christianity for the first time conceived of a complete union of religion and altruism, and since altruistic instincts are as old as egoistic instincts and biologically as necessary, Christianity thereby tapped a deep and permanent source of religious emotion. At best the other cults had merely suspected the necessity of this union; they had never made it their essential doctrine.

In this discussion it becomes necessary, of course, to view Christianity in the way a Roman would have done, a Roman who naturally did not accept its apocalyptic claims and who, as a member of a magnificent world-empire, was naturally suspicious of the doctrines advocated by conquered and despised nations. Christianity had come westward through settlements of Greek-speaking Jews, and a historian can hardly discuss the spread of this religion without giving great weight to Alexander's rôle in disseminating Greek in all of Western Asia, making it possible for the Jews who learned Greek to settle down during and after the Maccabean wars in every trading post of the Mediterranean. When St. Paul preached to the Galatians, for instance, he preached primarily to the Jews brought from Mesopotamia and settled by Antiochus in that part of Anatolia which Augustus annexed to Galatia shortly before St. Paul came there. Probably very few Celts of Galatia ever heard of St. Paul's letter. At Corinth, which Caesar had colonized with ex-slaves from Rome (i. e. a conglomerate chiefly of Greek-speaking Orientals), Paul found a city of freedmen and traders which had also acquired a large Jewish group. Paul's letter to the Romans (written, of course, in Greek) went to the Jewish colony, as we realize when we read its arguments based upon the Mosaic law. When Paul undertook to address native Greeks, as he once did on Mars Hill at Athens, he met with a very chilly reception.

Now, of course, Paul presently turned from the Jews to the gentiles, but it was among the mixed gentile colonies of the Greek and Roman cities, not among the old-stock Greeks and Romans, that he met with success. Such mixed peoples, brought up in their various cults, comprehended what he meant by "spiritual cleansing," "resurrection of the body," and "miracles," in a way that few Romans could. Corinth was wholly a conglomerate of ex-slaves; Philippi was a recent colony made up largely of the eastern contingents of Rome's army, and the Anatolian towns where Paul preached were mostly trading posts on the Royal Road that had been colonized by the Syrian kings and had recently, under the *pax Romana*, attracted many immigrants. Ephesus, the harbor town of that road, was full of Anatolian traders of every race.

Rome itself had an Oriental population of perhaps 500,000 or more when Paul reached the city as a prisoner two or three years before his death. He was there as a prisoner in chains waiting for a hearing, and it is hardly conceivable that citizens of the old stock should have come to hear him preach. Since, however, he was permitted to preach freely, Mark and Luke and other devoted disciples probably brought him such persons as they thought might prove favorable to the new doctrine. By their combined efforts it would seem that some thousand converts may have been won over in those two or three years. At any rate Tacitus gives the impression that the Neronian persecution in 64, in which Paul and Peter apparently fell, involved large numbers. It appears then that the Christian religion, like all the mystery cults, began to spread as the cult of a racial group, but that it very soon accomplished what none of the other cults could, namely, that it spread through propaganda outside its own racial group over all the other groups of about the same social standing, though not at first winning converts among real Greeks and Romans. Its diffusion, for over a century at least, seems to have been confined chiefly to the Oriental groups that the ordinary processes of Rome's expansion had scattered over the Empire. The converts in "Caesar's household" are, of course, of the same class, for the word "household" refers to the freedmen and slaves of the palace.

It is not difficult to imagine, even from a purely Roman viewpoint, what there was in this religion that would appeal to the laboring classes of Rome, to men who had grown up in Mithraic and Baal cults. The religious conceptions of Christianity were in themselves not strange to such men, the rites and sacraments (eucharist and baptism) were of a kind familiar to them, but simpler than those of most of the other cults. The promises of divine aid (immortal happiness with release from hunger, sickness, and labor) were far more definite and backed by far more documentary authority; not only were witnesses of the facts presented still living, but the Septuagint scriptures, with all their prophecies now apparently being fulfilled, presented visible proofs that no other cult could equal. Here, too, was a vigorous propaganda that claimed exclusive privileges such as no other cult possessed, and it was all conducted in Greek, the language of Rome's foreign quarters, whereas the rituals of other Oriental cults contained phrases in the languages of each group which prevented their being understood outside the group. Again, the Christians early formed into congregations for mutual aid and encouragement, and Paul, by writing letters to these congregations, started a custom which bound them together and made them conscious of their numbers. One must also mention Paul's wisdom in advocating liberalism. Being a Roman citizen who had seen much of the world he knew that it would not do to impose the exacting cult customs of any one race upon others. Non-Roman festivals, costly offerings, circumcision, peculiar food, the taboo on cheap sacrificial meat, and the rest, he simply eliminated from the essentials. Finally his Epistles were written to meet the definite and actual problems of each group.

We may assume that what St. Paul preached day after day to the crowds at Rome was the doctrine of the "Sermon on the Mount" and the story now contained in the Gospel of Luke. Those who have tried to understand the exacting ritualism of the other cults, and their disregard of spiritual values, will readily see that the new religion, with its generous humanitarianism, must have appealed to the miserable millions of the Roman Empire. One has only to visualize the crowds that lived in Trastevere in St. Paul's day and then read the sayings of Matthew to comprehend that a teacher as wise and enthusiastic as Paul could not but succeed there.

How the doctrine permeated upward from that stratum is an intricate problem. I shall mention only two points. Romans in high offices of state, conscious of their mastery of the world, may have admired meekness and non-resistance in their subjects, though hardly in their fellows. A Pontius Pilate would not readily have understood the point of view of Jesus. However, the Empire was a time of rapid social changes. The proud old nobility had practically disappeared before Nero's death, and the freedman class had filtered into the aristocracy with unusual speed through the civil service under the emperors of the first century. By Hadrian's day the great-grandsons of those slaves of "Caesar's household" who had been converted by Paul might well have become enrolled among the patriciate and might thus have carried the new religion into the higher stations. To be sure, it would be difficult for scrupulous Christians to hold high offices that required the employment of the official oaths, but some Christians adopted the Pauline formula of "all things to all men," while others retired from the civil service, and clung to their religion. It is also probable that Christian nurses and tutors in the great families were effective propagandists among the children.

Finally, the example of St. Paul in wisely adapting the Christian rites and doctrines to the varied temperaments of his different audiences was not forgotten. Christianity was not by any means uniform during the formative period. Except with regard to its fundamental tenets, it adapted itself to the needs and customs of the various nations. In the famine-stricken regions of Anatolia its preachers promised a heaven with ever-bearing fruit trees; for the overworked serfs of Egypt it provided refuges in monasteries; to the Berber mountaineers of Africa it gave a holy cause for crusading, especially against rich and oppressive landowners; to educated Romans, like Minucius Felix and Lactantius, it permitted the reading of Cicero and Vergil, nor did it attempt to deprive the real Greeks of Homer and Plato.

In short, the Oriental mystery religions, because of their restricted appeal, their national limitations, their burden of confused and incomprehensible rites, and their failure to prove morally valuable, seldom spread beyond the groups of immigrants to whom they were native cults. None of them had the capacity to become a world-religion. Whereas on the other hand, partly because of social conditions created by an extensive migration and by the rapid rise into high political and social station of such immigrants, partly because of a wise propaganda, and, of course, chiefly because of its central ethical doctrine, the Christian religion succeeded in permeating all classes of society in the Roman world in the brief space of three centuries.

FARMERS OR PEASANTS

HISTORIANS have with some dismay observed that even in the study of institutions as remote as those of ancient Rome personal bias or nationalistic preconceptions creep into the modern interpretations of past events. We have been more prone in America than elsewhere to place a high estimate upon the accomplishments of the agrarian society of old Rome; probably because we have had so large an agricultural population of rather high quality here. Jefferson, who based his political policy on his great faith in the farming class, was prone to attribute all successful government, ancient and modern, to this class. "Those who labor in the earth are the chosen people of God, if ever he had a chosen people, whose breasts he has made his peculiar deposit for substantial and genuine virtue." And it is still customary for our American statesmen to plead that the future of our country depends upon the stability of our rural population. President Roosevelt, for instance, probably was sincere when he said:

Upon the development of country life rests our ability . . . to supply the city with fresh blood, clean bodies, and clear brains that can endure the terrific strain of modern life; we need the development of men in the open country, who will be in the future, as in the past, the stay and strength of the nation in time of war, and its guiding and controlling spirit in time of peace.

Almost every president in his inaugural address utters similar phrases.

Perhaps as the rural vote diminishes in importance these sentences will dwindle in length and assurance. It certainly is true that our metropolitan weeklies are now less considerate of the sensibilities of rustics than a few decades ago and that a whole school of novelists has sprung up that thrives by satirizing the manners of rural communities and small towns. And the tendency is being projected into our histories of other and former cultures. The metropolitan praise of machine industry and of the urban life that accompanies it is holding up to view a new set of standards by which to estimate the success of past ages. Archimedes' screw and Hiero's royal vessel of 4,000 tons are displacing Plato's dialogues as measures of Hellenic progress, not only in the history of H. G. Wells but in those of certain very modernistic classical scholars. It is in the light of this trend that we can understand the favor that has been granted recent histories which generally speak of the Roman farmers as dull "peasants," measure Rome's success in terms of urbanization, and attribute the fall of Rome to a putative revolt of the "peasantry" against the bourgeoisie. In view of this strange turn in interpretation I have thought it worth while to discuss the question of Roman agrarian society, for it is my belief that the truth lies with neither of the extreme interpretations just mentioned but somewhere between. I also believe that no ancient civilization long survived the decay of its independent agrarian population.

The sociology of the agrarian groups of ancient Rome must be studied epoch by epoch, if we are to reach sound conclusions.[1] I shall first speak of the period before the great Punic War. At the time of the Twelve Tables Rome was a city covering about a square mile, with a rural area of about 300 square miles which contained several small villages. A few decades before this time Rome had temporarily prospered in commerce and industry under an Etruscan despot, but after his expulsion the citizens gradually settled back to the quiet life of a farm community.[2] The whole population numbered not over 125,000, a large part of whom lived inside of the city walls, although at least half of them were actual farmers. These men either went to their plots day by day or lived during the season of farm work in temporary straw huts on their small farms. Their villages were simply communities of farm folk, not, like ours, small commercial centers. A little over a hundred years later, the Roman state included more than ten times this acreage, for it had incorporated a large number of towns and villages as far south as Capua. But the social system remained as it had been. Farming — the actual manual work, I mean — was still the chief occupation of most of the men. They still dwelt in towns, generally going out to their small plots in the morning and returning at night. Plots of from five to ten acres were the rule under the hoe-culture of that day. If a village had a thousand farmers the area about it need not necessarily be over 10,000 acres, and no farmer need go more than two miles to reach his plot. Many farmers in present-day Italy go three or four miles each day to reach their small farms.

This situation is very different from anything that we know of in a land where farms usually comprise 160 acres, where in fact the owner lives on his land, and where farmers are therefore so isolated that the most serious concern of rural sociology is how to keep the agrarian families contented, how to hold the boys from drifting to the cities and the girls from the insane asylum. The old Romans never had to face such questions. They were sociable folk, but the village society answered their needs. It was possible for the women to spin, knit, and sew while gossiping together. The children had all the playmates they needed all day long; the men had companionship at evening and probably also in the fields. On market days they would go to the city,— Rome or Tusculum or the nearest market place,— barter and talk crops and politics to their hearts' content. The cities also celebrated several annual festivals and had elective and legislative assemblies which all the farmers were expected to attend. There they came into touch with the affairs of a larger world. In fact they had the free social life that English and French peasants enjoy today, besides the independence and interest in their own land, their work, and their government that American farmers generally have. We must call them "farmers" and not "peasants," and at the same time recognize the fact that they lived in a more natural society than our rural folk do. And this is doubtless one reason why the Romans so long clung to their favorite occupation of farming, why they never took extensively to industry and commerce, and why their cities grew so slowly. Today it is often said that the intelligent go to the cities so that the farm folk gradually deteriorate by a natural selection of the less ambitious. Whether or not this is true, we do not notice the same tendency at Rome.

However, this "Jeffersonian society" did not last forever throughout Roman Italy. Rome expanded rapidly, partly because this very farm life raised a sturdy stock of men who, when the state became involved in warfare, fought with a power and determination that resulted generally in victory. We also know that the birth-rate was relatively high, so that the desire for new lands may have injected determination into the right arm that drove the spear point home when there was war. In almost every instance of victory, some portion of land was confiscated and colonized so as to provide a self-supporting barrier of Roman farmers against hostile attack. Thus a series of forts was raised that cost nothing in the upkeep, land was found for the surplus population, and centers of Romanization were placed among the Italic tribes. The policy of this state of farmers was by no means stupid, and, measured by the standards of the day, was unusually liberal. It concerned itself wholly with land. It kept Rome agricultural in the same way that our expansion westward kept us agrarian in the early centuries of our republic. And Rome's expanding stock was not a "peasantry" in the sense of that word as it is usually applied to the small tenant farmers of Europe.

The policy, however, had unforeseen consequences that became apparent in the Catonian and Gracchan period. During the expansion through Italy the booty in metals, land, and captives had been moderate. With the Hannibalic and Macedonian wars, however, which were fought on a gigantic scale, there was a change. In the first place, the state, unable to find colonists for the devastated lands of southern Italy, resorted to an extensive plan of renting out public lands. Many Roman farmers took profitable leases of several hundred acres which they turned into slave-worked ranches and plantations, and the foreign victories supplied them with slaves at low prices. Thus large-scale absentee farming and ranching entered Roman economy. Secondly, the protracted wars had worked as an economic catalytic, driving many farmers to bankruptcy and giving a chance to the shrewder or more fortunate ones to accumulate estates. Immediately after the Second Punic War those who had lent money to the government demanded repayment so that they could invest their cash in lands that were then cheap. Some fortunate investors combined several lots into villa estates of a hundred or two hundred acres, and, buying slaves for a hundred dollars or less per man, they went into capitalistic farming. Thirdly, a few of the fortunate generals reserved for themselves enough of the booty to invest in large estates — a custom as well recognized then as it was in our own navy during the Civil War. The result of all this, during the fifty years of Cato's era, was that in many parts of Italy, especially in Etruria, Latium, Campania, and Apulia, slave-worked plantations and ranches were bringing good returns to gentlemen farmers who lived most of their lives in Rome, and that fairly large numbers of the less fortunate farmers, who could not compete with their stronger rivals, migrated up to the Po Valley or into the other provinces to begin life anew.

The story of this vital change has often been told, and at times with some exaggeration. It is a very serious mistake to assume that it affected all of Italy, or to say that capitalistic slave-agriculture had become the normal economy for all of Italy in Cato's day. Our own agricultural enterprises are on such a vast scale that we are prone to interpret vague phrases about the growth of plantations in terms of our own huge areas. We must, therefore, do some defining. These Roman estates were in fact rather small when viewed from later rather than from previous experience. The olive plantation which Cato discusses comprised less than a hundred and sixty acres and employed only thirteen slaves. And he could not manage the olive-gathering or the pressing with his own staff. He let that work out to a contractor who brought in a troop of fifty free folk to do the work. It is also quite possible that Cato's orchard was the only large one of his neighborhood and that there were scores of small farmers in the community who were glad to work for pay during the olive harvest when general farmers had little to do. Of course, there were many large olive and oil plantations like Cato's in Campania and Latium, for these products were more profitable when handled with some capital, with an accurate knowledge of methods and of marketing, and with a saving in overhead expense. But there were still many moderate plots in Italy then; modern France and Italy prove that olives and wines can still be profitable in the hands of small producers. We know that cereal raising and truck farming never fell into the hands of the large-scale producers at Rome.

Again, the census statistics show that, while the small farmers decreased in number during the period of increasing slave economy, the decrease of free citizens was by no means so great as to prove that the small producer had disappeared. The increase in population was normal between 200 and 163 B.C., then for thirty years there was a drop in the number of able-bodied male citizens from 337,000 to 317,000, after which there was a normal recovery. The fact is that we hear of very few millionaires during the whole period of the Republic. Romans of native stock seldom engaged in lucrative occupations like commerce, banking, and industry, which were socially taboo. Very few proconsuls had as yet — like Verres later— returned from exploited provinces with pockets crammed full. The most successful generals and administrators, men like Scipio, Paulus, Cato, and Sempronius Gracchus, died relatively poor. The stories told by Polybius of the difficulties their families had in providing dowries for their daughters reveal the fact that Rome still thought in frugal terms. Sums of $25,000 were spoken of as very large. In 160 B.C. it was still possible for the Roman Senate to pass a law [3] limiting the cost of banquets to one dollar.

Nor did the richer landlords increase greatly in numbers or wealth during the last century of the Republic. During the civil wars many wealthy landowners suffered from the proscriptions of Sulla and of the triumvirs, who especially needed land on which to colonize their soldiers. The colonization projects of Sulla and of Octavian resulted in a considerable division of latifundia into small lots. It has been reckoned that at least half a million such allotments were made in consequence of the civil wars. [4] To be sure, many of the soldiers who received such bonuses were urban drifters who made but poor farmers, but there were also sturdy folk among them. The soldiers to whom Augustus allotted land had largely been drawn from the farms and many were glad to return. Among them were his own troops recruited in Campania, ten legions that Caesar had levied chiefly in the Po Valley and Narbonese Gaul, and the several legions that he had recruited in Italy during his march on Rome or had drafted in the Italian levy of 49. There were also the legions that Ventidius had collected in northern Italy and the troops that Hirtius, Pansa, and Decimus Brutus had recruited in Italy. There is no question that the resettlement of such men on several hundred thousand small lots enlarged the percentage of the small farmers in Italy.

And finally, although the latifundia had spread to some extent over Roman Italy in Cato's day, the rest of the peninsula, comprising about two thirds of the whole, had been less affected by capitalistic farming. In the part of Italy which won citizenship through the social war of 90–89, villages of independent small farmers were everywhere in vogue. That here a large population of free folk still existed is shown by the fact that the census of Augustus in 28 B.C., the first efficient and full census after the incorporation of all of Italy in the state, reveals a very large increase in the number of citizens over that of the Gracchan census. Italy, except for the lands near Rome and in the south, was still on the whole a land of small farmers. There were now many more wealthy landowners, of course, and some vast estates in Italy, but during the last decades of the Republic landed investments had been placed to a greater extent in Spain, Gaul, and Asia than at home. The millionaires of whom we now hear with some frequency had generally grown rich by following the flag into the provinces; there they had bought lands at low war-prices, taking advantage of their knowledge that Roman peace and consequent prosperity would follow Roman administration. They had learned, we may add, that large estates in Italy were more liable to confiscation than those abroad, since in times of civil wars Italian allotments were usually promised to soldiers.

There had also been a reversal of feeling against slave economy in Italy, partly because of the slave revolt under Spartacus, partly because statesmen like Caesar had learned to appreciate the fact that a vast empire could not be ruled without the backing of a sound and healthy stock of citizen farmers. Caesar, in fact, had a law passed requiring that at least one third of the farm and ranch labor must consist of free citizens. This law seems to have been difficult to enforce, and it apparently fell into abeyance after Caesar's death, but it marks a veering of official opinion against slave-worked plantations. We know from other sources that rich landlords began about this time to make a practice of leasing out their estates instead of employing slave labor. On the whole then, although we find that large estates were still fairly numerous in Italy in the days of Augustus, the tendency toward concentration had met with several checks and the small farmers of the old stock continued to be numerous throughout the peninsula and especially in those districts that had been incorporated in 89 B.C. Vergil's splendid tribute to agriculture was intended for the actual practical farmers who wielded the hoe and the pruning hook:

Laudato ingentia rura, exiguum colito.

The Georgics barely take cognizance of the gentleman who lives in the city and only occasionally visits his stewarded estate.

The attitude of the Roman writers toward the farmer's occupation would cast some light upon the nature of the rural society were it not for the fact that political and economic motives as well as satirical overtones were apt to enter into such documents. Every time a presidential message or campaign speech reiterates the time-honored praise of the "sturdy and clearthinking farmer," my fellow-townsman, Mr. H. L. Mencken, takes another fling at the "rustic boobs." Somehow farmers belong to the class of necessities — like mothers-in-law, fathers, wives, and adolescent youths — that has furnished Aristophanes, Martial, and Punch with their thirteen standard topics. Such joking is not to be taken too seriously. In the Roman farces the farmer had a constant rôle. Cicero, when he is not talking before the general assembly, is apt to let fall uncomplimentary remarks about the dull wit of the rustics, the *agrestes*. It was Cicero more than any one else who determined the respectable connotation of our word *urbane*, by constantly using it as an antonym of *rustic*.

But this stock joke is by no means universal in Latin literature. The technical writers on agriculture, men like Cato and Varro,[5] are exuberant in their praises of farm life, and in their writings they refer not only to the casual visits of wealthy landlords to their estates but also to the practical vocation of farming. Cicero exhibits the traditional Roman point of view when he holds that agriculture is the one respectable occupation for a Roman gentleman, since banking and industrial and commercial occupations are tainted by low ideals. Vergil, who wrote his Georgics with the small farmer constantly in mind, knew well enough the hard work this occupation demanded, but his enthusiasm for its wholesome independence and the charm of rural surroundings constantly carried him into ardent paeans. "Carefree quiet, and a life ignorant of disappointments, wealthy in manifold riches; the peace of broad lands, caverns and living lakes, cool retreats, the lowing of oxen, soft slumbers beneath the trees, these are always his; *there* are the glades and thickets that shelter the game, there youth hardy in toil and trained to simplicity, devotion, and reverend age; among them Justice set her last foot-prints as she deserted earth." That may be the sentimentalizing of a farm lad,—twenty years after he had forgotten the twinge of tired feet and calloused hands, — it may be "emotion recollected in tranquillity," or memory emotionalized in tranquillity after the pain had faded from strained sinews, but it does truly and sincerely convey the attitude of most Romans of the Republican period toward a respected occupation in which they had so large a share and interest. A very large number of the successful men of the time had in some sense been farm boys.[6]

Agrarian politics are often condemned as being shortsighted and selfish. Recent American histories have blamed the farmers for the Mexican War, and — by a process of logic hard to follow — even for the War of 1812. We associate the "Grangers" of the last generation with an unsound financial policy, and sometimes wonder what can be the conception of humanity in the group that advocates the debenture

and the "dumping" of our wheat on foreign markets.
Roman politics were largely agrarian till well past the
days of the Gracchi, though here we must distinguish
between the era of the dominant small-farmer and
the period when the capitalist landlord controlled
legislation. On the whole both periods reveal alter-
nate feats of myopia and of wisdom. Neither group
clearly understood economics outside of their own immediate interests. Rome was extraordinarily slow to
adopt a coinage, and though the Republic in general
held to honest standards it never evolved any elastic
or scientific currency system. The farmers also were
very stolid as regards commerce and industry. There
never seems to have been any proposal to protect industry by tariff or to grant any kind of monopolistic
favors, though the Romans knew that their neighbors
used such devices. Even when Sicilian grain came to
Rome in great amounts they accepted the competition with apparently no objection — though in this
case it may be that the agrarian region about Rome
had already taken to raising vegetables, wine, oil,
and cattle to such an extent that no distress resulted
from the import of grain. More striking is the fact
that when Gaius Gracchus was farsighted enough to
propose establishing a few seaport colonies that would
presumably aid commerce, his agrarian supporters
fell away so that he lost his election and his power.

In general, agrarian politics were conservative,
prudential, and unafraid of hard tasks that seemed
necessary. The farmer did believe most firmly in
property rights and was always ready to go to war

against lawless neighbors who did not respect these rights. And when he once entered a war, he was ready to fight to a finish — it was the other fellow who had to cry quits. And when the opponent quit, he had to apologize and give up a portion of good arable land to pay for his misdemeanor. On the other hand, the farmer had a certain sense of justice. He held to a rule — or at least he claimed that he invariably held to the rule — that he was never the aggressor in any war, that every time the assembly voted to fight it was in a just, defensive cause. Before an attack he also stated the cause and gave the opponent thirty days of grace in which to make reparations — on his terms. Furthermore, after the victory, which he was very apt to win, he usually offered liberal terms, that is, terms liberal for that day. Inside of Italy he did not pretend to subordinate the conquered. After indemnities had been paid, he would exact no standing tributes, he would accept the conquered tribe on equal terms in the Roman federation or as citizens in the Roman state. These Roman farmers apparently felt that the Italic tribesmen were very much the same kind of folk as they, and that it was prudent to have them as friends and partners rather than as persistent enemies. But this was a feeling that did not extend to foreigners beyond the seas. There is perhaps something universally agrarian about such a limitation of sympathy.

In Cato's day, when the gentleman farmer had become more powerful in the Senate than the small holder, we notice a gradual divergence of the farmers into two separate factions. The city-bred landowner had become educated, had read much foreign litera- ture, and was ready to take an interest in foreign politics. The Senate, in fact, voted to give aid to the Greek democracies against the tyrant Philip, but here the small farmers of the popular assembly op- posed the Senate. It took the senators some time to persuade the assembly to give in, but they finally succeeded. However, in the end the sentimental gentlemen found themselves unable to prove their policy a success and the ordinary voter insisted that either the foreign venture must be made to pay or it must be abandoned. The small agrarian had his way and the Senate had to take to practical politics.

The same spirit of *real-politik* soon mastered home affairs. The large farmers of the Senate wished to preserve the public lands for leasing — since they could afford to take leases and profit by them. The small farmers, who served in the armies, desired a distribution of these lands as soldier bonuses and as colonies for their sons. To be logical they should have advocated bonuses for their Italian allies as well, but on this point they insisted less. The result of the factional contest was a rather selfish compromise whereby moderate bonuses were given to some 40,000 soldiers, a few colonies were founded with small lots for citizens, a few Latin colonies with smaller lots were established for the allies, while the larger portion of public land was preserved for leaseholds. Here again we may observe rather characteristic agrarian politics.[7]

The two Gracchi, who were nobles and well-to-do, stand out quite apart from their class. They were large landlords, but men of deep reading and wide sympathies. They disliked slavery, not from any sentimental or moral objection to the institution, but because slavery resulted in the reduction of the sounder body of small farmers, a body which they thought that Rome needed. Tiberius Gracchus proposed to the Senate that the state limit leaseholds on public lands, compensate for the equity on excess holdings, and distribute the recovered lands in small lots to citizens who needed them. There were enough urban poor, semi-bankrupt agrarians and farm laborers desiring such allotments to make a success of the scheme. When the Senate voted against his proposal, he strained the constitution, disregarded the Senate, and asked the primary assembly to give him its support, and he carried the measure. This seems to me to prove that in the assembly, at least, the small farmers could still dominate legislation, if they chose. After the death of Tiberius, the Senate succeeded in clogging the machinery of allotment, and a few years later his brother took up the proposal. Gaius Gracchus cleared the way once more for a wide distribution of lots, but when he proposed new measures in aid of commerce and asked also that the assembly grant citizenship to the allied tribes of Italy, he lost the sympathy of a large part of his voters and met with defeat. Again we have an instance of the politics of the Roman farmer, who was quite willing to be just if it did not cost too much, but suddenly quite conservative if the proposed legislation offered expensive justice to a stranger or to a foreigner. In this case it was the large landlords who were the more obstinately egoistic.

The demand for citizenship for the Italian allies came up again and again. The poorer folk of the city were usually inclined to favor the proposal, probably feeling that the democratic rural element of the assembly would profit by the adhesion of most of the new voters. The senators in general opposed the measure, not desiring the assembly to become too strong for their control. Throughout non-Roman Italy the small-lot system still prevailed, and the new voters would quite certainly not favor the aristocracy. When the franchise bill was rejected, the Italians revolted, and, after a struggle of more than a year, they were admitted to citizenship. But the Senate tried first to restrict the new voters to a few wards and, not succeeding in that, prevented a full registration of the new voters. In fact, the civil war between Sulla and Marius began because of a quarrel over the question of whether or not the new voters should have a fair registration. Marius, a man of democratic sympathies, threw his influence in favor of an honest distribution, while Sulla led the senatorial objectors. And it was on this issue that large parts of Italy rallied to the support of the democratic leaders and made war upon Sulla and the senatorial régime. The aristocracy won by use of the army, and Sulla immediately abolished the censorship so that the Italian farmers to a large extent failed to win a chance to register for the voting privilege for which they had fought.[8] It was not till twenty years later that a compromise was reached and the censorship restored. The census was then taken, though by no means efficiently, and the old quarrel between the two groups began in a measure to subside.

However, the Italian farmers did not wholly forget their grudge. When seven years later Catiline proposed to lead a rebellion against the government of the nobility, he won support not only from the "hungry mob" of the city, the dispossessed, and the restless veterans, but also from the poor villages of rural regions like Picenum, Apulia, and the Praenestine areas, where the large estates had made threatening headway.[9] Catiline tried, with some deception, to reawaken the old hatreds between the great landlords and the small farmers whom Marius had befriended. Thanks to Cicero's leadership, however, the rebellion was scotched before it had spread far.

A few years later, when Caesar was on the point of crossing the Rubicon, Pompey uttered the foolish boast that he had but to stamp his foot and all of Italy would rise to the defense of the Senate. But Pompey, like most senators, was blind to the feeling of distrust that the landed nobility had awakened among the poorer farmers. The old animosities of the Marian day had not yet subsided among the sturdy rustics of Italy. Cicero, wiser than Pompey, knew that this element could not be relied upon by the Senate, though he hardly gave the correct explanation for their dissidence when he wrote that they were

unpatriotic enough to abandon their independence
provided they might live in peace.[10] Those farmers
were doubtless ready to fight for a reasonable issue,
but they were wise enough also to see that Caesar as
dictator would be more likely to protect their interests than a victorious aristocracy composed of
landlords. Pompey did stamp his foot, but in vain;
then he sent out recruiting officers to make forced
levies throughout the farm villages. In this manner
he got several thousand men enrolled, but the new
levies loitered listlessly till Caesar came up, and then
they deserted to him. They might very readily have
reached the Pompeian general, Domitius, who was
holding a fort in central Italy, but they had no desire
to; for Domitius was a haughty landlord whose garri-
son consisted largely of his own tenants forced into
military service at the master's orders.

In a word, the civil contentions of the forty years
from 90 to 50 B.C., which led to the fall of the Republic, reveal a serious gulf between the plantation
owners who controlled the Senate and the small
farmers of Italy who might have controlled the assembly if the state had permitted them an effective
machinery for the expression of their opinion. In the
end even Caesar deceived the small farmers. He began well by instituting a local census registration
throughout the Italian municipalities,[11] and the next
step obviously would have been to arrange for local
balloting on the candidates for Roman magistracies.
That at least would have given some meaning to
the franchise in the far-off country districts. But

Caesar was ambitious. He actually did not desire an effective democracy. He intended to do the ruling, and he did.

And that was the end of agrarian politics at Rome. At best it had revealed no great brilliance or statesmanship. The failure of the Republic is in the main chargeable to the large landlords. They had been too ambitious for power abroad and for opportunities to exploit the provinces. They had selfishly welcomed cheap slave labor without considering how they thereby crowded out independent farmers and bred up an incompetent and unpatriotic citizenry for the future. They refused to legislate in favor of a native industry and commerce that might have served as an economic buffer at critical times, and they generally kept the franchise as restricted as possible so as not to lose control of affairs. The small agrarians showed even less wisdom. They developed few competent leaders and followed these only intermittently. They abandoned Gaius Gracchus when he offered a program that compassed more than their material needs, and many of them accepted the dangerous leadership of Marius and Catiline, who were too vindictive and narrow-minded to secure the confidence of the majority. In favoring Caesar against Pompey their instincts were fairly wise, but the Republic was by that time doomed. Caesar meant to help them, but he never intended to use a democracy except as a throne for his own dictatorship.

Agrarian politics completely failed. But we must add that it failed after five centuries of amazing accomplishments. No republic had till then revealed such driving force, such a capacity to use its man power and material resources for the interests of the state. No state had developed a cleaner family and social life, a juster government of subjects, a greater respect for law and order, a sounder moral code, than this agrarian Rome as it was in the second century before our era.

The emperors seldom took a vital interest in the agrarian situation. Caesar, to be sure, outlined a plan to drain marshes so as to improve agriculture, and, as we have said, he tried to force plantation and ranch owners to employ free labor on their estates. This may have encouraged the movement, that had already begun, to manumit slaves and give them leaseholds. The triumvirs and Augustus confiscated many large estates of the senators who had opposed them, and they allotted these lands in small parcels to their soldiers. But the process of estate-building continued unrebuked, even if the tendency was now to substitute renting and subrenting for slave-economy. As peace continued, fewer cheap slaves appeared on the market, and the rental system sometimes proved to be more profitable than the exploitation of expensive slaves who frequently resorted to sabotage. However, the slaves did not all disappear from the farms. Columella, who lived in the middle of the first century, assumed that slaves would be used by the viticulturists for whom he wrote, and Pliny's letters refer time and again to slaves used by landlords as well as by contract renters.

Because the recruiting of legionaries in Italy ceased for the most part after Vespasian's day, modern writers frequently assume that small farmers were then very scarce. There is no doubt that the Flavian and later emperors saw the need of saving the Italian stock, and there is evidence enough that it was dwindling. We may also surmise that large landowners brought pressure to bear upon the government not to levy their renters for army service. We had numerous examples of that type of patriotism in America not so long ago. But there is also evidence of the continued preservation of the small plots. Several of the villas excavated near Pompeii [12] consisted of only a few acres, and Columella repeatedly speaks of five-acre vineyards. Moreover the famous mortgage tablets of Beneventum and of Veleia near Piacenza, which together list about one hundred farms, give us some useful information about their size.[13] Though the number of possessors listed on these tablets had shrunk from 181 to 100 in a century, nevertheless few of the farms were large, in fact only seventeen per cent of them covered more than fifty acres, the other eighty-three per cent ranging from five to fifty acres, and averaging about twenty-seven acres. What is more striking is the fact that the best farm land, that of the valley districts, had largely remained in the hands of small possessors, while only in the pasture lands of the hills had there been a striking tendency to aggregate several small plots into single ranches. If these two tablets could be considered representative for the period around A.D. 100, we should have to assume that the small farmer held his own with remarkable tenacity on the good arable land, and that he had yielded only before the capitalistic cattle-raiser of the upland districts. However, both of these tablets came to light in rather remote parts of Italy which the Roman landlords had not penetrated to any extent. What we may reasonably conclude from them is that in a large part of the hilly country of Italy the valley villages of petty farmers remained fairly safe from the encroachment of latifundia.

The later Empire was a dismal period for the poorer farmers of Italy, for practically all, whether tenants or small owners, gradually fell into serfdom. There have been many guesses as to how this happened, but they must remain guesses because most of the records of the period written at the time when it was happening have been lost. The prime cause seems to have been the misrule and anarchy of fifty dismal years during the third century.[14] Throughout this period the barbarians were breaking over the border everywhere, necessitating indiscriminate recruiting of troops from any place where men could be found for the army. These soldiers, chiefly uncivilized provincials, were out for adventure and plunder. When they failed to get their pay — and that happened frequently — they foraged and robbed, or they raised one of their favorite officers to the throne, one of their kind, of course, usually in return for promises of a bonus. At times there would be three rivals for the throne. Civil wars resulted, and, while the rivals fought each other, the frontiers were exposed to barbarians. The economic machinery went to pieces; commerce and industry dwindled. Taxes rose because the troops demanded higher pay, while everywhere profits with which to pay taxes were diminishing. Several of the usurping emperors, when in hard straits for funds, levied upon cities and temples forced loans which were in fact confiscations, and finally resorted to the open confiscation of public and even private goods. Of course taxes on the land were the first to rise. Leaseholds became unprofitable because the taxes took too large a part of the whole yield. Renters accordingly began to desert their tenancies rather than work for nothing. Accordingly, when the emperors found the taxes dwindling, they invented the rule that tenants must respect the terms of their leases or be subject to arrest, and in time — we do not know the date — all the holders of land-leases in Italy were declared life-tenants and their heirs were compelled to continue the leaseholds. They were not serfs in every sense of the word, but they were as hopelessly bound to the land as serfs.

By the middle of the fourth century this amazing social revolution had taken place throughout Italy. Nor were the poor freeholders in a much better condition, for they too, ground down by the heavy taxation, found that the only escape from ruinous debts was to accept the protection and "patronage" of rich and influential landlords, and this eventually placed them in the class of the bound tenantry. By the time the consequences of the anarchy were over, the state, through confiscations, and the influential landlords who had had power enough to resist ruinous exactions owned the larger part of the arable lands of Italy. The independent small farmer had fallen into serfdom.

In this brief talk I have attempted to sketch what seems to me the fortunes or misfortunes of the Roman farmer from the early days when the very men who wielded the mattock also administered the affairs of state until that later day when the man with the hoe became a serf without any influence in the community. I have felt that it was urgent to survey conditions thus because most of our Roman historians are Europeans who have seldom seen farmers as anything but tenants, or ex-serfs or peasants, and are not apt to reach spontaneously the correct connotation that such words as *agricola*, *rusticus*, *agrestis* contained in a simpler rural polity. In saying this I have in mind even so brilliant a book as Professor Rostovtzeff's *Economic and Social History*, a book that I value above all others that have been written in my day on the subject of Roman history. It is a masterpiece; but the author's references to the Roman "peasant" I venture to think would have been altered here and there had he ever had the privilege of studying the lives of a normal group of actual farmers. He speaks for instance (p. 47) of the Italian farmers of the Augustan day as "half free," a statement that I do not comprehend. Then he employs the phrase (p. 51), "the urban, that is to say the civilized element." Vergil was a farm lad and certainly came from a civilized stock. A little later we find the idea reiterated in these words (p. 82): "the civilized portion of the Empire, the city residents." This attitude one finds in most of the continental histories, and it generally leads to an overemphasis of the magnificence of what the authors call "capitalistic farming" and a failure to estimate the number and influence of the average farmers. The tendency reaches its real danger-point in the tenth chapter of the great work to which I have referred, where the author explains the anarchy of the third century as due to a contest between the oppressed peasants and the urban "bourgeoisie," as though the army was a kind of communist troop of peasants trying to wipe out capitalism. We know, of course, that a large part of the disheveled armies of that day had been recruited in the Balkans, in Anatolia, and in Africa, but that does not make them "peasants," nor is there any trace of a peasant class-consciousness among them. They were farmers and craftsmen, shepherds and laborers, and not a few were bandits from the Balkan mountains. The inscriptions and papyri which are cited to supply the evidence for this thesis happen to speak chiefly of how the poor farmers of Asia, Egypt, and Thrace suffered from the foraging parties of these very soldiers as they passed through.[15] The soldiers were as ready to steal grain from peasants as from other men. And Herodian, who is the chief source for the period, remarks that in the raiding of the cities the soldiers themselves objected to being made the tools of forceful confiscations by their generals.

These sources in fact picture only the outlawry that always arises in any protracted period of anarchy. It was not a class contest between peasants and cities.

In this brief sketch I have tried to trace the behavior of agrarian policies in a great agricultural state of the past. We have found in them a tendency toward myopia and narrowness, a certain fear of thinking in telescopic terms, but we have also seen therein a sound kind of conservatism, a respect for hard duty, a penchant for fairness, balance, clean morals, and independence that created a very great Republic. The greatest danger to that Republic came through admitting slavery into the state, a policy which did so much to thin out the population of normal farmers. We are also in danger of losing from the fabric of our national life the sound fibre contributed by our old farmer stock, though here, of course, the cause lies not in slavery but in the attractiveness of urban life and in the rapid spread of that capitalistic and co-operative farming so loudly praised by our metropolitan economists. Historical parallels are seldom safe guides, but they may be employed as suggestions to thought. President Hoover, in his first message to Congress, said something to the effect that agriculture was not only an economic problem, it was also a mode of life. That was also the view of the great Gracchan reformers. Had they won the Senate to their doctrine Rome might well have avoided autocracy.

IV

ROME'S EXPERIMENTS IN
SOCIAL REFORM

W E HAVE long known that democratic governments are slow to adopt plans of social amelioration and that paternalism often makes more rapid
progress under autocracy than under popular rule.
Forty years ago Imperial Germany was setting a
pace in providing old-age pensions, higher national
education, and employment insurance that France,
England, and the United States could not even re-
motely follow. One reason for this apparent paradox
seems to be that a strong central government, un-
hampered by frequent changes of administration, can
plan and execute vast programs; another, equally obvious, is that governments which repress political
liberty must, in order to protect themselves from
revolution, provide compensation in the form of economic and social confections. In America, conforming
to the spirit of our polity, we have been peculiarly
averse to forcing our government to assume non-
political burdens. We dread national ownership and
operation, educational supervision, participation in
world courts and the vast programs that delight dic-
tators. Despite the rebuke of the "progressive"
weeklies we continue to elect presidents who advo-

cate laissez-faire individualism. But our instincts in doing so are comprehensible in the light of history.

Natural man objects to restraint. Psychologists have told us that the child has only two instincts at birth: he does not like noise,—unless he makes it,—and he insists on his god-given right to kick when any one tries to hold him. When we shape governments, we make just enough rules to keep the political machine going. We are instinctively averse to burdening ourselves irrevocably by obligations and ownerships.

I have employed this old truism by way of preface, because, when I trace the efforts of the Romans toward social reform in a few experiments, you may care at the same time to notice how changes in the form of government affected the scope of their social thinking. Under the Republic they were even more dilatory than we, but later their emperors gradually learned to be over-bold, and finally launched into the most thoroughgoing state-socialism that the western world has ever known. That ended in complete disaster.

Let me add that I do not intend to dwell on theoretical proposals such as we find in Cicero's *Commonwealth*, in the essays of Seneca, that drawing-room reformer, or in the gospel of sentimentalized and emollescent Stoicism found in the *Thoughts* of Marcus Aurelius. It is more interesting to see what the Roman government, conducted by practical men, tried to do from time to time in the field of social amelioration, and in the economic and juristic changes that had some social purpose. That is the more appropriate since the Romans, so like the English, found their way through deeds rather than through formulae.

When the Latins emerged from obscurity, they were a group of self-governing communities in which "popular sovereignty" was unquestioned, and the individual citizens, gathering in town-meetings, decided their own affairs very much as did the New England settlers in their town-meetings. They were what Aristotle used to call "political animals." The history of five hundred years of republican rule is in a way unlocked by that key-fact. During those centuries the Romans threw off every dictator who tried to impose himself, they responded willingly to every call for self-defense, but they refused to burden themselves with costly standing armies; they disliked to encumber the state with anything like permanent charitable and educational institutions, if the individual or family could assume such burdens. The people were so fearful of powerful corporations that no form of mercantile combination was permitted, much less encouraged, as it has been in Europe. Monopolies could not arise except in the very few instances permitted by the state for purposes of collecting the revenue. Class legislation was prohibited, paternalistic schemes frowned upon, trade was free, Roman seas and ports open to all; individual endeavor was favored and protected from state interference as well as from unduly powerful combinations. In fact, Mr. Hoover's essay advocating individualism would have been well received by the Roman citizens of the Republic as containing their basic philosophy of social and economic aims. (Not till the populace was displaced by immigrants unaccustomed to self-rule, so that monarchy became imperative, did social legislation find a large place at Rome. Then Augustus began tentatively with a series of reforms which in time transformed Rome. I shall have to confine my illustrations to a few of the institutions that were affected by the political changes in Rome's long history.

In a previous lecture I have said that the old Roman family was monogamic and secured merely by a simple contract.[1] It was not till canon law of the church made its way in the paternalistic empire that marriage became a religious sacrament — as it is still supposed to be in Spain and in Maryland. In most nations today marriage is considered a civil concern. In the Roman Republic, characteristically enough, marriage concerned neither state nor religion. It was simply a contract between the persons involved, witnessed by the responsible members of their families. And, as we should expect with the growth of individualism, such witnesses in time lost their constraining authority. At the end of the Republic annulment of the contract by mutual agreement sufficed in law, and finally even the annulment of the contract by a casual announcement on the part of one. The result of such action was that the Roman family seemed for a while to disintegrate, but during the Republic no one proposed any remedy.

However, it was only a few years after the Monarchy

had displaced the Republic that Augustus proposed a series of drastic laws designed to check what seemed a great danger to the social order. To be sure, he still refused to consider state interference with divorce. What he tried to do was to induce marriage and the increase of offspring by a series of penalties and awards. Unmarried men were declared ineligible for certain offices of state, were liable to special taxation, and were not to have the privilege of seats in public theaters and games. There were similar penalties for divorce, and the statutory cause for divorce might be recognized in civil courts as a crime if any one cared to prosecute. Since such laws led to unfruitful fictitious marriages, they were followed by a promulgation of rewards and penalties to increase the birth-rate. Such laws, modified from time to time, remained upon the law books through the Empire, though seldom enforceable. Since few would go to the trouble of prosecuting, they had little direct effect. Finally, the autocratic Christian emperors of the late Empire, aided somewhat by the foreign doctrine of the Old and New Testament that woman was somehow a creature of inferior rights and subject to stricter moral rules than man, placed marriage under church supervision and laid down the divorce statutes that have held till recently.

There is a tradition among historians that charity is a virtue of the highly civilized. The student of ancient history lands in difficulties if he tries to proceed on that theory. Biology, in fact, seems to show that altruism and egoism are based upon instincts equally old and that both are virtues equally necessary for survival, and equally dangerous when allowed to operate in excess of reason. Just because Christianity discovered how well the altruistic instinct served as a foundation for religion, we must not assume that it did not exist before. It did, but it expressed itself in other forms. The historian of Rome, if he is at all concerned with moral values, does well not to measure the evidence of the instincts themselves, but rather to evaluate the prudence that is applied in a wise political direction of these instincts. And from the point of view of statesmanship the greater degree of prudence is usually called for in altruistic legislation for the very reason that society profits immediately from, and therefore gives a heavy premium to, social goodness. In fact, society often demonstrates its selfishness by over-rewarding the social virtues.

During most of the republican period the state took little interest in problems of charity. Indeed there was little need, because, as in America till about 1880, there was then enough public land available for settlement, so that a large indigent class did not exist in Rome until Cato's last years.[2] During the second century the rapid spread of the plantation and slave systems threw many small farmers out of their possessions and the city of Rome accumulated a large class of needy citizens. The Gracchi then proposed colonization on public land for the indigent of Rome, but the argument for the proposal was chiefly political. It was urged that the free rural population must be increased in order to insure a sound body of citizen-voters and of strong soldiers for the armies. As a temporary makeshift (probably meant to cover the interim till colonization could be perfected) Gaius Gracchus also instituted the bread-line. The poor were given tickets for wheat at low prices (as all nations did during the Great War — England is still giving doles). Later the Gracchan colonization plan was repeatedly proposed but regularly opposed by a government that refused to acknowledge the theory that the state must care for the needy.

Here again it was autocracy which attempted to face the question in all seriousness. Julius Caesar colonized very widely and diminished the doles in order to entice men to the colonial plots. But his colonization was far more than an eleemosynary institution. Caesar chose his colonial site with a view to developing those parts of the empire that especially needed reënforcement.

Augustus may be said to have invented a new system of aids. His large standing armies were open to those who were out of work and found no means of support. After twenty years of service each veteran was either settled on land or given a bonus from the treasury with which to acquire about five acres of arable land. This indirect colonization through army service succeeded so well that it became the favorite expedient of his immediate successors.

One of the most extensive state charities known to history was organized by the emperors Nerva and Trajan.[3] Then as now rural folk were too widely severed to form effective organizations for self-pro-

tection; they were among the first to feel the need of
governmental aid and the last to get it. Italian lands
cultivated intensively for centuries were suffering
from erosion and over-cropping, marketing facilities
were meager with the tardy methods of transportation
of that day, and small farmers with deficient means
were suffering severely from the competition of richer
landlords who could diversify crops and command
the available markets. A protective tariff directed
against the products of the new provinces could not
with reason be invoked to aid the farmers of Italy because the provinces were also a part of the Empire and
claimed equality of treatment. In consequence the
free population of Italy was dwindling and there was
much poverty. In addition to humanitarian arguments for relief, the government comprehended that
the safety of the borders that ran through thousands
of miles of barbaric country would ultimately depend
upon the maintenance of a solid population of reliable
folk near the center.

These emperors, therefore, resorted to direct state
aid. Two objects were aimed at. One was to give
rural credits, that is loans on farm mortgages at the
low rate of five per cent (an institution not unlike
the Federal land-banks which we created a few years
ago). The second object was to extend charitable
pensions to needy parents of children in order to
stem the decrease of the birth-rate (an institution
which some of our state governments, like Pennsyl-
vania, resurrected a few years ago under the name
of "motherhood pensions"). The two institutions

were organized under a single imperial board with local subcommittees operating in every community throughout Italy. The funds — probably not far from a hundred million dollars — were taken wholly out of the state treasury and distributed to the committees which placed the mortgages where needed. The annual interest sums accruing on these mortgages were not returned to the central treasury, but were collected by the committees which, in the capacity of charity boards, distributed them to parents to be used in the rearing of their children. A hundred million dollars may seem a small sum, but it was in fact more than twice the annual revenue of the state, and the burden on the state would, therefore, equal an outlay of at least six billion dollars on the part of our Congress. It is probably the most costly charity scheme ever devised.

It would be worth much to know what were the results of this vast humanitarian plan. Unfortunately most of the literature of the period that followed perished in the dark ages, and in consequence we are left in almost complete ignorance. However, no remarkable change seems to have taken place, because a century later, a time from which we have considerable knowledge of Italy, we still hear of the same poverty and of a dwindling population. And in the third century when, like the German mark after the war, the denarius lost its value, all trust funds, including this, evaporated. To us the experiment is of interest in showing that the government of the Empire had completely abandoned the laissez-faire doctrines of the Republic, had felt constrained to assume the burdens of social as well as political welfare, and had studied the problem enough to see the close connection between economics, social well-being, and political salvation. This kind of paternalism was, however, a concomitant of autocracy, not of democracy.

After Trajan's amazing experiment the emperors hesitated at no project of economic or social purport, so far as the treasury seemed able to endure the strain. In order to understand the outcome, it is well to sketch briefly the constant enlargement of legislative scope at Rome. The Republic, as we have said, instinctively avoided paternalism. It never interfered with, nor gave state aid to, trade, manufacturing, maritime commerce, or agriculture. The individual was expected to solve his own financial problem. While Carthage had endeavored to procure a monopoly of trade for her own merchants in her colonial harbors, Rome never did. All nations were treated alike. Carthage had kept a fleet to protect her trade routes and to sink foreign ships that dared enter her lanes through the straits of Gibraltar. Rome advocated open seas and did not, except intermittently, keep a sufficient fleet to police her seas against piracy. Though the eastern kings protected their merchants and producers by giving various monopolistic privileges and by protective tariffs, Rome exacted very low tariffs,—not over five per cent,— and only for purposes of revenue. And though the old Roman farmers suffered from competition with every new province that opened up to agriculture under the Roman peace, those very farmers apparently never asked the state for protection.[4] What is even more surprising, while Roman citizens, subject to the restraints of Roman corporation law, could not form joint stock-companies to promote their industries, the provincials — who were allowed to operate under their own laws — could form such companies, and could therefore organize stronger mercantile associations and invade the Roman and Italian markets to the disadvantage of home production. This was laissez-faire with a vengeance.

With the revolution that introduced autocracy this aversion to state interference gradually vanished. Julius Caesar, as soon as he became dictator, began with large plans of state control, and though he died too soon to execute them, they reveal a new theory of political obligation. He began by designing aid for commerce. A Tiber canal, a good public harbor for Rome at the mouth of the Tiber, a canal through the Isthmus of Corinth, Roman harbor colonies at Carthage, Corinth, Sinope, and elsewhere were surveyed. Rural Italy was to be aided by the drainage of marshes, the building of roads, not only for military needs but for traffic, and by the decree that free labor must replace at least a third of the rural slave labor. This program reveals a new trend in government, which, however, the immediate successors of Julius hesitated to follow boldly. But in time the emperors did follow.

When on the defeat of Antony and Cleopatra Augustus took over Egypt, he did not banish state-ownership, which was intrenched there, though the system was so repugnant to the Romans that he kept the province virtually severed from the rest of the empire. Claudius carried out several of Caesar's plans, and took a new step in granting state insurance to shippers who placed their vessels at the service of such carrying trade as the state needed. Domitian attempted a drastic reform when by decree he limited the planting of vineyards in favor of cereal culture throughout the empire, and, what was more daring, favored Italian culture by imposing severer restrictions on the provinces than on Italy. This last measure, however, was felt to be unjust and was presently revoked.

It was during the second and third centuries of the Empire that the activities of the government were extended to the point that endangered solvency and that finally led to the restriction of all individual initiative. The so-called "good emperors" of that period were strongly moved by humanitarian ideals. As we have seen, Nerva and Trajan gave lavishly to charity when it might have been wiser to invite the loyalty of the provinces by reducing their taxes. Emperors like Hadrian, Antoninus Pius, and Marcus Aurelius seldom knew when to stop in attempting to aid the sluggish elements at the expense of the taxpayers. They did not confine their interests to Rome by any means. Backward cities in Africa, Spain, Greece, and Asia were given funds out of the state treasury with which to carry out the ordinary work that the municipalities themselves had formerly cared for. Water systems and aqueducts, sewers, temples, free public baths, city-halls and other public buildings, parks, schools, roads, harbors, market-places, shady porticoes, theaters, and gymnasia were erected from state funds by imperial architects all the way from London to Bagdad, from the Alps to the Sahara, though it had formerly been the duty of local organs to do these things. The imposing ruins of the Roman imperial structures at Merida in Spain, of Timgad in Africa, of Baalbek in Syria, will remind you of the extent of such work.[5] Only a few years ago Athens borrowed money in New York to replace with a new water system the aqueduct that Hadrian built and gave the city one thousand eight hundred years ago.

Needless to say, such undertakings depleted the treasury and compelled the emperors to raise taxes to the limit of the taxpayers' capacity. The results were unfortunate. When in the next century the barbarian invasions began, against an unprepared and depleted government, and taxes had to be raised still further, the confusion of sedition and unpreparedness led to civil wars that lasted for fifty years, driving the state ever deeper into bankruptcy.

The emperors unable to meet their obligations resorted to compulsion. In the rural communities, when the overtaxed renters threw up their leaseholds in despair, they were ordered by edict to remain on their rented farms for life, and when their sons fled, a new edict compelled sons of renters to take up the leases of their fathers for life. The state needed the taxes regularly. This was the beginning of a new serfdom instituted for the alleged benefit of the state. Property owners were compelled to accept the responsibilities of municipal office and assume the burden of making up the deficit in local taxes year by year, so that they, too, were bound to state-service so long as any property remained. The urban population fared no better. They were compelled to join appropriate guilds which in turn were forced to give service to the state at call; and sons had to join the guilds of their fathers. Here, too, all individualism vanished. The citizens of Rome with their children were tied to their occupations; they had lost their economic and social freedom; all were bondsmen at the call of the state. The Bolshevik committee that rules Russia can alone supply a parallel to this régime in its control over the lives and properties of all citizens of the nation.

How had it all come about? Far back, was the thoughtless expansion of the Republic that made an empire too cumbersome for a republic to rule, and the admission of such hordes of slaves that Rome's old population, which had always insisted upon self-determination and individual rights, gave way in time to a docile mass that was willing to trade away self-government for bread and games. It was over-expansion that had made a monarchy necessary, and a non-Roman population that permitted the monarchy to slip into an autocracy. But what finally happened was what one may expect of autocracy (even when it is benevolent) as compared with republics. When the government began to assume the task of directing and aiding individuals and communities in production and in trade, in education and in public work, in charity and in amusements, the primary aims of administration were neglected, the burdens upon the taxpayer passed all bounds, and for self-protection the state was compelled to enchain every citizen and make of him a cog in the universal machine.

One would hardly suggest that experiments in state-socialism are condemned by the failure in this case. The crisis at Rome due to the racking strain of barbarian invasions was very unusual, and the men who — like Diocletian and Constantine — conducted Rome's experiment without having the advantage of history to warn them, plunged entirely too optimistically into the cavern. However, the results in this instance seem to be worth pondering. At least it is apparent that the suspicions of the earlier Republic that paternalism involved serious perils were well founded and went back to a prudent human instinct which is still of some validity.

It is frequently said that republics are incapable of governing subject peoples. The statement is based upon historical parallels that may prove invalid, because it is now possible to awaken very quickly the public conscience of a nation to protest against misgovernment. Success in the government of subjects depends in some measure upon the existence of sympathetic paternalism, and for that reason the Roman Empire, which failed in so many respects, succeeded somewhat better for its first 200 years in governing provinces than did the Republic.

It must be admitted, however, that while the state was relatively small the Republic did remarkably well. For some reason the older Romans showed an unusual respect for law and a capacity for good government. It is not an accident that no one volume outside of the Bible has had as wide an influence as the Roman code, and history can show no parallel to Rome's first four republican centuries of progressive political reforms accomplished without violence in primary assemblies. After the first wars of the fourth century B.C., the Roman citizens revealed a liberalism toward the defeated that was unheard of in other ancient nations. The defeated were not then made to pay tribute. They were all permitted local self-government, the nearer ones made full citizens of Rome, the others included in a federation bound to mutual defense. Indeed the striking success of the early Republic in foreign affairs can be explained only by the loyalty of the federal members that was deservedly won by Rome's willingness to recognize the instincts of individualism in her subjects as in her own citizens.

The same concern for the rights of the individual appears in the early Roman court. When in the early Republic foreigners began to put in at Rome's harbor to trade, it was noticed that many misunderstandings arose because the foreigners did not know Rome's laws of contracts. In 242 B.C., therefore, in order to attract foreign trade, Rome instituted a special court for foreigners the duty of which was to settle disputes, not according to Roman law, but according to the customary practices of the foreign traders, the prac-

being or equal or fair

tices of other nations, that is, the *jus gentium*. Through the rulings of this court the Romans soon inferred that civil law was not final, that equity should be the aim of all law and in fact stood over and above statute. As a result, the Roman courts not only began to revise the code by the substitution of customs learned in this court, but also to attempt to find a basis in equity for all their court rulings. This process continued till the assumption was made that the instinct for justice was universal, that in fact there was a "natural law," universally applicable, based upon human nature, and that all local codes must somehow find a foundation, not in local needs and desires, but in the laws of nature.

You will remember how very differently Greek philosophers reached the same conclusion about the same time. When Athens lost her liberty and became subject to Macedonia, her Stoic philosophers for the first time discovered that all men ought to be brothers, that it was unjust for one people to hold dominion over another, that there was a natural law of equity to which all human laws should conform. The Athenians adopted a humanitarian political theory in order to tame the harshness of their conquerors, but in Greece it remained a bookish doctrine, forgotten by every government that exercised power. The doctrine of equality has very often been the defensive gospel of the under dog.

Rome had found the doctrine not through the application of a philosophic theory, but through prudent experiments in administering subjects and in shaping an appropriate court for strangers. That court is one of the very startling things in history. A century before the Romans knew anything about Greek ethical thought, at a time when Rome had as yet not a page of literature and long before any Roman had put into writing any formulation of legal principles, the Senate created this court, which put into practice all that Stoic philosophy could not force into the law books of Greece. Two centuries after that court was instituted, Cicero, in one of the most masterful paragraphs in all literature, formulated its implications in terms that were also acceptable to Stoic theory: [6] "True law is right reason consonant with nature, world-wide in scope, unchanging and everlasting. . . . We may not oppose or alter that law, we cannot abolish it, we cannot be freed from its obligations by any legislature, and we need not look outside ourselves for an expounder of it. This law does not differ for Rome and for Athens, for the present and for the future, but one eternal and unchanging law will be valid for all nations and all times. . . . He who disobeys it denies himself and his own nature."

It is beside the point to say that we have now rejected the underlying philosophy of this doctrine. That does not invalidate the statement that the paragraph has wrought greater progress in jurisprudence for nearly two thousand years than any other written statement of the same length. What I have wished to illustrate by the reference is the characteristic fact that the Romans acting on a truly democratic instinct put into actual operation a principle which was not adequately formulated in words for centuries.

You will not read far in Rome's code before you run into numerous axioms like these: "The study of law concerns itself with discovering what is just and unjust." "Law is given by nature: animals as well as men have practices based upon natural instincts. Marriage is a natural institution common in some form to all living creatures." "The rights of natural relationship, no statute law can destroy." Much of this is cast in Stoic phraseology because the later jurists were Stoics, but the foundation lies throughout on native republican juristic practice. Even the preamble of the "Declaration of Independence" with its questionable assertion of "natural rights" grew very directly out of that law. It was the institution of the peregrine court in 242 B.C. that begot Jefferson's phraseology.

The Roman Republic, therefore, had laid a very sound foundation for world-wide administration. However, when expansion spread very far from Rome, the Republic lost touch with more distant subjects and failed, as we should expect, to create an adequate administrative machinery for them. In a republic, remote public duty is apt to be no man's job. Business men, looking to their own interests, began to exploit the unguarded subjects, to "develop the natural resources" of the provinces for their own pockets, to place loans at high rates of interest in the Nicaraguas and Cubas of that day, and to involve the provincial governors in their schemes. In the last years of the Republic there was much underhandedness, much placing of secret and oppressive contracts,

much irregular exploitation, and at times much loot-
ing. Republican administrations of short duration
were no match for shrewd business agents who were
always on the job, and officials, who were working
temporarily in the public cause and for a public that
was far distant, shut their eyes to half-concealed ir-
regularities. The last century of republican provincial rule was more than a failure in Asia, Syria, and
Spain.

It is, of course, not quite fair to say with Lord
Cromer that the idea of benefiting the governed did
not occur to them. That sentence is wholly false. It
rests partly on a mistake of Mommsen,[7] who misinterpreted a phrase of Cicero, and partly upon the bad
record of the last century of the Republic. As we have
seen, even the Republic in its early days assumed that
subjects had a natural right to equitable treatment.
And the idea never died even in the days of worst misrule. When, for instance, Quintus Cicero went to
govern the Asiatic province as proconsul, Cicero
wrote his brother in a letter of advice: "Those who
are in charge of provinces should make the happiness
of the governed their *only* concern." And he makes
that statement time and again through his life, especially in the letters written from his own province.

However, the republican government was unable to
cope with the problem of a wide empire in Cicero's
day. The emperors, who could assume large responsibilities because of their long tenure, were the first to
do away with the abuses of the late republican governors. Even Caesar, who had not been too scrupulous

while a republican official in Spain and in Gaul, began
to consider the needs of the provincials as soon as he
became dictator. He reduced the tribute and introduced an honest system of tax-collecting, he reformed
the administrative methods and he extended civil and
half-civil rights into the provinces so generously that
all believed the day near when practically the whole
empire would be placed on a par with Italy. Succeeding emperors usually appointed honest and considerate governors, and even autocrats like Claudius and
Nero, who tyrannized over the Senate at Rome, usually had the good sense to invite the good will of the
provincials by keeping efficient governors in charge.
And what was of very great importance, the practice
of respecting autonomy and the local customs lasted
over from the Republic long into the Empire.

The earlier Roman emperors intervened but rarely
in provincial affairs.[8] They insisted on peace, and let
the provincials work out their own cultural salvation.
In Gaul, for instance, the provincial borders were protected by imperial forces and such roads were built as
were necessary for the preservation of order. The
Gauls paid taxes to aid in this necessary work, but in
all else they were let alone. No attempt was made at
first to have the Gauls give up their tribal organizations and substitute Roman forms of government;
there was no demand or request that the Gauls adopt
the Latin language, Roman customs, or Roman religion. Non-interference was the rule. And the results
of that liberalism were startling. The Gauls of their
own accord hired teachers from Rome and estab-

lished schools. They were soon visiting Rome to acquire her ways, reading Roman books, building Roman villas, and entering the Roman civil service. In the fourth century Gaul was producing more of Rome's literature than the whole of Italy. In fact, the whole of Gaul was Romanized in three centuries of non-interference more thoroughly than Bretagne, a later Celtic enclave of Gaul, has been converted to French speech in fifteen hundred years of French rule. Laissez-faire has had some very great successes.

Thus far I have dwelt upon the willingness of the early Empire to continue the republican policy of non-intervention in provincial society while assuming only the burden of honest government. This policy, however, could not endure, since autocratic supervision permeated every department of state in the fourth century. The "good emperors" of the second century began by intervening with acts of uninvited kindness, the bad ones of the third intervened in the interest of higher taxation, and in the fourth the imperial masters of the treasury, the diocesan overseers, and the spies were everywhere. Autonomy was then at an end, and imperialism had run its normal course when state supervision and "state socialism" spread over the whole realm.

Religion had a similar experience at Rome. During the Republic, as we have remarked, liberty of conscience was respected, as is so frequently the case under polytheism. Every man could worship or not worship as he chose. The state had a recognized list of deities that were accepted as official by a board of fifteen senators, and this board would determine whether or not a temple might be erected within the city walls. But the decisions affected only the official cults in which the state participated. If the board found no reason for acceptance, the temple could find a place outside of the walls and the board did not undertake to interfere with individual worship. Only once during the Republic did the administration undertake to check the spread of a religion, and in that instance the objection was to immoral practices, not to the creed.[9] During the Republic we hear of no other suppression of cults, except the removal of illegal shrines from within the walls, though in Cicero's day hordes of slaves were brought in from Anatolia, Syria, and Egypt with a great number of strange orgies that must have been distasteful to the staid priests of the Roman cults.

Here, too, a change came with autocracy. Augustus set an example in religious intervention by revising the authoritative list of cults and giving state aid to the rebuilding of the temples of all the accepted ones. Presently he organized a new official cult of "Rome and Augustus," which later autocrats made use of to test the loyalty of subjects. After that, religious persecution was not far off. After the great fire of Nero's day, in order to stem the rumor that Nero had caused the conflagration, some official, who had heard that the Christians prophesied a general catastrophe of the world, suggested that the Christians might be the guilty ones or might at least serve as scapegoats. Some Christians were examined, and it was then discovered that their doctrine forbad among other things offerings to the official Roman deities. They were pronounced traitors to Rome, a judgement that could not have been pronounced by any court during the Republic. The first great persecution of Christians followed, and thereafter until their religion won official recognition no Christian was immune from the charge of treason. Autocracy had once more proved its proneness to carry paternalism to a consistent end.

Again, it was not till autocracy came in that the state took a hand in public education. During the Republic teaching rested with the family. Mother and father both devoted themselves to the task of teaching or chose tutors to do it. Naturally private schools sprang up in great numbers, and in Cicero's day there was little evidence of illiteracy. However, the state did as little for education as in England before the nineteenth century. The question had been raised as to whether Rome should not undertake the task in some such way as Sparta had done, but Cicero in the *Commonwealth* probably gave voice to the standard Roman opinion when he said that uniformity was undesirable and that the Spartan schools at least were unable to fend off immoral practices. The old Romans had reason to show faith in the family.

Rome never went in heartily for public education, but the Empire made at least a fair beginning. Caesar began by inviting foreign teachers to Rome by a promise of citizenship — then difficult to procure — and by projecting the foundation of a great public library. Caesar did not live to see this library completed, but Augustus built two, bought books very extensively with public funds, and appointed competent librarians whom he placed in the civil service. Succeeding emperors increased the number to at least nine, and Hadrian spread the public library service as far as Athens and Timgad. Public university education at Rome may be said to begin with Vespasian, who selected a number of teachers to lecture at Rome on state salaries of about $5000 per year. Hadrian reorganized this service into a permanent Athenaeum, and henceforth public state and municipal institutions of learning spread rapidly throughout the Empire.

We may add that literary patronage by the state had a similar history. Patronage of some kind was needed, since there was no copyright law and no printing. Hence books could be copied at will and consequently authorship could hardly be very remunerative, except for dramatists who could sell their wares to those who produced plays at festivals. During the Republic the authors were therefore apt to be men of competence, like Cicero and Catullus, or poets like Lucretius who caught the fancy of some private patron. With the Empire state aid appears. Augustus, and his minister Maecenas, who made it a custom to assume far wider responsibilities than had the former governments, procured pensions for Vergil and Horace in the form of landed estates; and from that time many an author successfully applied for state support.

These are only a few illustrations of a natural trend in administrative psychology. And I have mentioned them quite as much to illustrate human behavior at Rome as to give examples of a natural diversity between republics and autocracies. In our day republics were taught by the royal governments of Europe to broaden the scope of government from the mere task of administration, to accept some of the duties of social amelioration. A school of sociologists quickly arose which urged us to turn our government into a general eleemosynary institution. State universities were urged to become universal service stations to farmers, cheeese-makers, miners, laundry-men, and nurses. Our Congress is asked to set the price of wheat, distribute doles in Arkansas, procure manganese for Pittsburgh, and standardize our educational system. History warns us that republics with elective officials of brief terms cannot well accept too heavy a burden, while autocracies are all too apt to bury themselves in such commitments. Fortunately we have not yet a parliament of the world that might standardize all into one type. There are scores of governments providing apotropaic examples of what is too much or too little, and from them we shall doubtless be able to learn how to steer the safe middle course. But so long as we are a republic we may do well to remember that at Rome at least the saner statesmen had great faith in the capacity of the individual and of the family.

V

SOCIETY AND LAW IN EARLY ROME

THE study of Roman Law requires so varied an
equipment that no man can now be expected to
master the whole field. America has made very few
independent contributions in the subject, and the
English and continental scholars who have worked so
fruitfully at it have usually had to confine themselves
to a relatively small part of the range.[1] The philolo-
gists have been interested chiefly in ferreting out the
interpolations that have made their way into the
Code. The papyrologists have done excellent work
by way of revealing how Greek law influenced Roman
administration during the Empire. Those who have
had time for comparative jurisprudence have here
and there interpreted obscure lines in the early fragments by referring to practices in vogue elsewhere.
The historical researchers have clarified many passages by providing a picture of the social and
economic conditions that gave the impulse toward
certain types of legislation. But it stands to reason
that no man can adequately cover the whole range of
Roman law, history, and philology, besides mastering
Greek law, the vast bulk of Greek and Latin inscriptions and papyri, not to speak of the wide reaches of
comparative jurisprudence. The students of law have

accordingly specialized, and they have more and more given their attention to the imperial field in which new materials have come to hand. The law of the republican period has consequently suffered some neglect.

Here I wish to make some suggestions regarding the standard interpretations of early Roman law. Our chief source is, of course, the fragmentary quotations from the decemviral code made by later writers and diligently collected by scholars like Schoell, Bruns, and Girard. It cannot be said that these men have evolved objective criteria by which to determine precisely what to include in an edition of the fragments of the Twelve Tables. The Roman authors who cited lines from these tables sometimes abbreviated what they found in order to concentrate attention upon a relevant point. At times they took the liberty of inserting interpretative phrases which it is difficult for us to eliminate. Such phrases were sometimes added because the original language was no longer readily understood, sometimes because legislation, court decisions, or commentators subsequent to the Decemvirs had expanded the application of the original lines. So, for instance, the original clause that penalized the use of magical incantations [2] was subsequently interpreted as covering libellous literature and was therefore quoted with explicative additions; and the phrase *partes secanto*,[3] which apparently referred at first merely to the division of the proceeds of a bankruptcy sale, was misinterpreted by classical jurists as permitting creditors to carve up the body of a delinquent debtor. Hence, in editing the fragments, modern scholars have always had some difficulty in deciding which phrases to accept as original, and which to reject as interpolated. They have often had to base their decisions upon *a priori* conceptions of what early law was likely to be, and these conceptions have usually been deduced from a study of comparative jurisprudence, from a rather liberal use of classical law, and from statements appearing in standard Roman histories, frequently obsolete.

Now, to consider these aids in turn, the current anthropology of comparative jurisprudence is contaminated, it seems to me, by a perverted form of evolutionistic theory which scholars in other fields are abandoning. Only three decades ago we were overrun by schematized histories of civilization which were packed with concatenated phrases like "predative — pastoral — agrarian"; "alogical — prelogical — intelligent"; "savage — barbarian — civilized." And the various stages of culture were supposed to be discoverable in every tribe known to history. The patent fact that a people could frequently be alogical in religion while wholly intelligent in practical affairs was disregarded. That the human race had existed hundreds of thousands of years before the reign of Romulus, that cultural stages could be leaped over in times of migration or by fortunate contacts, that primitive customs might spread laterally by diffusion from the outside as well as descend by survival, that some peoples could have started their progress in thinking so many thousand years before historical times that all legitimate basis for the comparative study of their evolution was beyond reach, that what seems primitive among Hottentots might be the result of thousands of years of decadence — all this was pointed out in vain. The persistent evolutionist insisted upon compassing the progress from our most distant ancestors to the glories of the Ford age in a single formula. He talked as though Homer had just bid farewell to a grandfather who hung by his tail from a Thracian oak tree — Homer, whose exquisite sensibilities and delicately poised distinctions are still the despair of translators. There is, I dare say, a greater mileage of progress from the yelp of a savage to a canto of Homer than there is from a paleolithic artifact to an airplane.

The chief error involved in employing classical law as an aid in interpreting older legal customs derives from a proneness to map out a consistent line of development from a hypothetical primitive law to the developed code of Justinian. Yet no law develops in a straight line in all respects. The law of the Twelve Tables does not contain a consistent social conception. It embodies some very crude religious practices, as when it hands over to Ceres any destroyer of standing grain. On the other hand it is very liberal in the matter of inheritance. It is probable that the Tables contain a conglomeration of old Italic village practices, some liberal customs that arose when Rome under the kings enjoyed an extensive foreign trade, and also various ideas which the Etruscan princes had inherited from Hittite and Mesopotamian laws.

Furthermore, it is probable that when the law was codified it was passing through a transition stage. The firm prohibition of costly funerals and of the burial of gold jewelry and rich robes with the corpse points very clearly to an attempt of the Romans to get rid of recently imported Etruscan burial customs and to revert to native Latin usage. The Etruscans in this matter had conserved practices that belonged to an old Asiatic conception of post-mortem ownership (*Totenteil*) for which the Latins had no use. Similarly, the emphasis in the Twelve Tables upon the cumbersome ritual connected with the sales of real estate (*res mancipi*) indicates a partly nationalistic desire to conserve old customs of the Latian farm against foreign methods of transacting business that had grown up in the city under the foreign rulers. In a word the Tables reveal many conflicts between old and new, native and foreign, urban and rural practices, and accordingly we have no right to look for a uniform cultural level in the code.

There are instances enough of inconsistencies in modern law to suggest that even where culture is fairly homogeneous the law may reveal unevenness. At the very time when Justices Holmes and Brandeis are issuing opinions that look to a vast reform of our legal concepts, Maryland still refuses to legalize civil marriage and still retains the use of the whipping post. Will future students eliminate all the evidences of cultural progress from the codes of today, simply because our court records have occasional references to witch-cats and Dayton trials? That is the method that has often been employed in editing the Twelve Tables. It has been a serious flaw in our editors of the early code that they have been so ready to eliminate from it whatever clauses seemed inconsistent with an integral preconception of its contents. It is not at all unlikely that the growth of a strong aristocracy after the code was made worked toward conservatism in the law of property so that in some respects there was retrogression rather than progress from 450 to 150 B.C. We know, for instance, that in England during Tudor days the testamentary law was more "primitive" in appearance than it was under the Roman rule over 1200 years before; feudalism had intervened and caused a regression in the practices of individual property-holding. The demand for consistency in legal history must be abandoned.

Finally, students of early Roman law have often employed an obsolete conception of what Rome was like at the time of the Twelve Tables. Though our knowledge of early Roman history has been revolutionized since 1900 by the discoveries of Italian excavations, students of law still seem to be drawing their pictures of early Rome from the old histories written before the new revisions were made. For example, in attempting solutions of the difficult passages of the Twelve Tables that deal with sales, debts, and contracts, they are prone to accept the conception of early Rome that Mommsen formed over seventy years ago, an interpretation that no longer corresponds to the known facts. Our older historians supposed that the Romans who wrote the Twelve Tables were just emerging from very primitive conditions where barter was the custom, where family ownership of land was just passing out of use, where personal property in land was a very recent innovation, and where foreign trade had hardly been heard of. The students of Roman law, who are filled with these conceptions, usually interpret the clauses of the Twelve Tables accordingly, eliminating as later interpolations all phrases that seem to imply more advanced economic conditions. But we now know that the ancestors of the Romans practiced orderly agriculture in the Terramara settlements more than a thousand years before Rome was founded, that they had had large towns in the Villanovan settlements of Tuscany for many centuries, that several decades before the code was made, Rome, ruled by a vigorous Etruscan prince, was the wealthiest city of Italy north of Magna Graecia, possessed the most extensive walls of any city north of Tarentum, splendid buildings including the largest temple in Italy, an active commerce with all the trading peoples of the Mediterranean, a populous group of artizans, Greek artists and builders, and a strong and well-organized army.[4] In fact, selling and buying had been ordinary transactions in Europe thousands of years before Rome was founded, as is clear from the fact that the Sanskrit and Greek cognates of Latin *venum* have the same meaning as the Latin word. Civilization was old long before the Twelve Tables were written.

It is impossible to harmonize the traditional legal interpretations of property, sales, and contracts found in the standard books on Roman law with our present-day conception of early Rome. We must ask the students of law to modernize their ideas of what Rome was like in 450 B.C. and to reinterpret their fragments in the light of this new knowledge. If they will do so, I think that they will see the importance of some citations that they have neglected and will be ready to give a literal translation to some phrases that they have been prone to explain by forced interpretations.

To indicate the direction which our revision of old interpretations will probably take I shall consider a few clauses of the earlier laws that deal with contracts, wills, and the family. In doing so I would especially call attention to the fact that the first code was in some respects advanced, that it was an inconsistent conglomeration of ancient native conceptions, foreign ideas, and of practices that had grown up under a striking social upheaval of recent day, and finally that it was shaped in a period of transition so that it was bound in some respects to show progress, in others retrogression.

In the matter of sales our most definite statement in the Twelve Tables [5] refers to *mancipium* (Table VI, 1, *Cum nexum faciet mancipiumque, uti lingua nuncupassit, ita jus esto*; When a contract or transfer is to be made, what the tongue has pronounced so the law shall do). The sale by *mancipio* was, of course, relatively infrequent because it was obligatory only in the case of *res mancipi*: land (with its servitudes), slaves, and cattle. The transaction called for five witnesses and a weighing out of the price in bronze (or a symbolic act representing the actual payment). As land could not be held except by *cives*, or by the Latins, who had access to the court, this ceremony, confined to the native population, could and did continue long in the rural districts.

The sentence is, of course, by no means explicit, and it is one of those that receive their interpretation largely from the interpreter's conception of what Rome's economic and social conditions were like at the time. The main question connected with the passage is whether such transactions must be completed at once by a transfer of goods and price or whether more liberal forms, as, for instance, of credit transactions, are to be assumed in the phrase *uti lingua nuncupassit*. Now, in a passage of Justinian's *Institutes* (II, 1, 41), which unfortunately modern editors fell into the habit of placing in Table VII, thus removing it from its proper place as a comment on the articles of the sixth table, we are explicitly told [6] that the Twelve Tables permitted the satisfaction of the vendor by pledge or guarantee in place of immediate payment. That would seem to be clear, but Karlowa (*Röm. Rechtsgeschichte* II, 612) set the habit of saying that this clause could not have been applicable at the time of the Twelve Tables to sales of *res mancipi* because Rome was then too primitive to use sales on credit, and Kübler's recent hand-book (p. 51) agrees with him. Girard (*Manuel*, pp. 290 ff.) does indeed accept it for *res mancipi*, but on the erroneous supposition that coinage was already in vogue in the fifth century.

In denying the appositeness of the clause it is customary to insist upon a very narrow interpretation of the phrase *uti lingua nuncupassit* (VI, 1). One school holds that these words referred only to verbal utterances as contrasted with written agreements; another that, since Festus (L. 276) quotes the phrase in connection with *pecunia*, it was applied only to the precise sum named as the purchase price. Neither interpretation is in any way compelling. The emphasis may equally well have been upon the word *uti*, and the most obvious meaning of the clause is that the parties to the transaction were to be bound by the agreement as spoken and witnessed by the five bystanders, whether it be a cash or a credit transaction. So far as this passage is concerned it rather implies than denies sales on credit, and in view of the clause quoted from Justinian it must be so taken.

Another favorite argument against an early date for credit transactions is the *a priori* assumption that the ritual connected with sales of *res mancipi* was not liberalized until coinage came into vogue. But the formality of the *libripens* had certainly become a symbol connected with credit-sales even before, since Varro [7] quotes the phrase *raudusculo libram ferito* from *veteribus mancipiis*. The use of *aes rude* preceded coinage by many centuries, and there can be no doubt that the use of one piece of *aes rude* in the transaction is symbolic and implies that the price is not of necessity immediately paid. Why not accept all the fragments that we have and read them at face value? Why insist that the Roman sale was more primitive in form than the language implies?

Those who have worked over the archaeological evidence of early Rome as it has come forth in recent excavations can have but little patience with the conservative interpretation of the Twelve Tables that assumes Rome to have been only a farm village. We now possess the remnants of at least fifteen well-decorated buildings of some magnificence erected at Rome before the time of the Decemviri, and much evidence of vigorous labor guilds and of foreign trade. Historians now generally agree that the first treaty with Carthage [8] was made about sixty years before the code was posted. This document proves that during the Etruscan régime Roman merchants had traded freely in the Punic parts of Sicily and Libya while the Carthaginians had traded as freely at Rome. The Cassian treaty of the Latin league (dating from about forty years before the code) assured the continuance of *commercium* between Romans and Latins and laid down the interesting provision that disputes regarding private transactions must be settled within ten days in the court of the city where the transaction took place. This would seem to imply that trade might rest on something else than mere simultaneous *traditio* by way of simple barter. Furthermore, the clauses of the Twelve Tables that deal with the rate of interest, with *nexum* and with *depositum* all point to contracts quite beyond the sphere of mere and immediate exchange of goods.

In a word we must assume that at the close of the regal period Rome was a large and busy commercial city where the old and simple forms of barter based upon the instantaneous exchange of goods no longer sufficed, and that merchants trading at Rome introduced many of the liberal forms of contracts that were in vogue at other ports. To be sure, there may have been some retrogression toward old Latin practices before the Twelve Tables were written, as in fact there was thereafter. But there is no reason why all the clauses quoted from the Tables in connection with the laws of purchase and sale should not be accepted at face value. They seem, it is true, to be more liberal than some of the clauses of a later day, but there are adequate historical reasons for assuming that trade retrograded rather than progressed during the decades that followed the decemviral legislation. In fact, after the Etruscan princes were expelled from Rome, foreign commerce almost ceased for a time, and building operations dwindled to meager proportions.

My second illustration is taken from the fragments that pertain to wills and legacies. According to the old Latin custom, if a man died without making a will, his property was divided equally between those who became *sui juris* at his death, that is, his widow and his children. There was no suggestion of primogeniture or of preferring sons to daughters.[9] The most important phrases regarding inheritance that are quoted directly from the Twelve Tables are the following:

Tabula V, 3 (according to the reading given in the two earliest quotations of it, *Auctor ad Herennium* 1, 23, and Cic. *De Invent.* 2, 148): *paterfamilias uti super familia pecuniaque sua legaverit, ita jus esto.* (As the father shall order concerning his estate so the law shall do.)

Ibid. 4: *Si intestato moritur, cui suus heres nec escit, adgnatus proximus familiam habeto.* (If he dies without will, and no heir of his exists, the nearest agnate shall have his estate.)

In the first of these quotations the wording is probably correct so far as it goes, though it probably omitted the clause *tutelave suae rei* which occurs in Ulpian fr. 11, 14, and in Paulus, *Digest* 26, 2, 1. The shorter forms of the clause, which omit *familia* and substitute *suae rei* (Gaius 2, 224; Pomp. *Dig.* 50, 16, 120) or *de sua re* (*Nov.* 22, 2 pr.), are late, and the substitution is clearly due to an attempt to modernize the clause after the word *familia* had become ambiguous. We know now that in early Latin the word *familia* meant the same thing as *res*, that is, the estate.[10] This passage should therefore be quoted as it appears in the early republican citations, and not as it appears in the works of later writers who omit *familia* or substitute latter-day equivalents for it. Whatever is to be said of testamentary rights under the Twelve Tables, the law apparently made no distinction in this matter between real estate and movable property.

A more serious question arises as to whether the second clause cited above (Tab. V, 4: *cui suus heres nec escit*) implies that if the testator has a *suus heres* he cannot deprive this heir of his portion even by will. Now legalists are wont, in discussing this question, to assume the existence of a primitive Rome

which was very near to community or family ownership of land when these laws were written. Mommsen's history, for instance, has left us a legacy of
statements like these: "It was not in the power of
the father arbitrarily to deprive his children of their
right of inheritance," and "Since the arable land
among the Romans was long cultivated upon *a system
of joint possession*, and was not distributed until a
comparatively late age, the idea of property was primarily associated with . . . estate in slaves and cattle
(*familia pecuniaque*)." These misstatements are, of
course, partly based upon an etymology of *familia*
that we now know to be incorrect. Furthermore, very
few historians now believe that there was a "system
of joint possession" in early Rome. Private property
in land seems to have been known even to the far-dis-
tant ancestors of the Romans who, several hundred
years before, lived in the Terramara settlements of
the Po Valley. We believe now that Roman landlords had for centuries bought and sold, accumulated
and frittered away landed property. We must also
bear in mind that during the Etruscan régime, at
least, there had been not a little "capitalistic" exploitation of large estates as is shown by the traces
of an extensive drainage system in various parts of
Latium. All property had for a long time been fluid
in the market, and any interpretation of these clauses
that is based upon the hypothesis that the Romans
were just emerging from the economy of primitive
village communities in 450 B.C. is apt to be erroneous.

Now Pomponius says: [11] "Verbis legis XII tabularum his 'uti legassit suae rei, ita ius esto' latissima potestas tributa videtur *et heredis instituendi et legata et libertates dandi* tutelas quoque constituendi." (By the words of the Twelve Tables 'uti legassit, etc.,' it appears that the widest latitude was given in instituting heirs, in bestowing legacies and manumissions, and in forming guardianships.) This statement is generally questioned, partly because of the misconceptions handed down by Mommsen's history and partly because later law is found to contain several restrictions on a man's power to bequeath his property. For instance, the *lex Voconia* was passed in the second century to prevent an estate from going out of a family through a female line, and later the *lex Falcidia* was passed to protect the putative rights of the natural heirs.

The truth of the matter is that the trend of Roman law in inheritance was actually away from the early testamentary freedom toward restriction, just as it was in medieval Europe under the feudal system. The trend was toward protecting estates and keeping them in the hands of those members of the family who had to bear the burden of civic obligations for the family, a trend that is natural in aristocratic society.[12] In the early Republic, after a long period of commercial activity had removed property from communal restrictions, it was wholly reasonable that land, like other property, should have been at the complete disposal of the *pater familias* as it had been in Mesopotamia eighteen centuries before. And as *patria potestas* was still so strong that the *pater* had complete power over the life of his son, it is hardly conceivable that at this stage of property-rights he did not also have complete power over his property. If he could legally condemn his son to death, he doubtless could also disinherit him. I can therefore see no reason why we should question Pomponius — who had access to the complete text of the Twelve Tables — in his statement that the *pater* once had complete liberty as regards the making of wills and legacies. The customary neglect of this statement of Pomponius is due to a general misconception of the direction that the later law of property took during the development of aristocratic power and government.

Similarly there is another ceremony, that of *coemptio* in marriage,[13] that seems to be misinterpreted, though in this case the cause of error was a misplaced anthropological theory. It will be remembered that there were in old practice four different forms used in marriage: (1) *usus*, whereby free marriage became a formal marriage with *manus* by cohabitation for a year, (2) *confarreatio*, a very formal marriage with religious sacrifices, for a long time employed by some of the patrician families, (3) *coemptio*, in which the formalities of *aes et libra* — ordinarily used in sales and testaments — were employed, and (4) *free marriage*, in which there need be no ceremony except that of mutual consent and in which the husband gained no legal authority over his wife. Classical law usually concerned itself only with free marriage and with *usus*, which were the surviving forms. *Confarreatio* and *coemptio* were defined by the jurists of the Empire but were spoken of as generally obsolete.

Now marriage by *coemptio, per aes et libram*, employed a ceremony that survived for a long time in making sales. In formal sales the buyer, in the presence of five witnesses, the seller, and the holder of the balances (*libripens*), touched the scales with a penny or a piece of copper which represented the purchase price and uttered a formula to the effect that he claimed as his the property in question for which he paid this price. When such a ceremony was employed in marriage, even though the formula was different, lawyers like Gaius naturally drew the conclusion that the rite was a survival of a bride-sale, and, inevitably, modern jurists who work with the materials of comparative institutions have readily acquiesced. Here, they say, in Roman practice is a survival from pre-Roman times when wives were purchased.

This conclusion seems to me far from convincing. In the first place, in early Latin the word *emo* meant to *take* or *accept*, not *buy*, just as our word *purchase* in Old English meant *seek* or *pursue*, not *buy*. There is as yet no proof that the word *coemptio* had anything to do with a purchase in early times. Secondly, there is no other trace of bride-purchase in Roman records, whereas the word *dos* (dowry), which is very old, as the form shows, implies a practice quite the opposite of buying the bride. Again, the act of *coemptio* is sometimes attributed to the woman [14] as well as to the man and sometimes to both the man and the woman, in both of which cases the phrase agrees with the early meaning of the word. Furthermore, the formula, according to Gaius,[15] was not the same as in the case of purchase. Finally, if the ceremony had ever implied a contract of sale, we should expect the maiden's father to receive the piece of bronze from the groom or from his father. There is no indication, however, that such was the case. Boethius,[16] citing Ulpian as his source, says: "Coemptio vero certis sollemnitatibus peragebatur, et sese in coemendo invicem interrogabant, vir ita; an sibi mulier materfamilias esse vellet. Illa respondebat velle. Item mulier interrogabat an vir sibi paterfamilias esse vellet. Ille respondebat velle." (In using the ceremony of *coemptio*, the man asked the woman whether she wished to become a *mater familias*. She answered "yes," and in turn she asked him whether he wished to become a *pater familias*, to which he answered "yes.") These mutual questionings seem difficult to reconcile with the idea of bride-purchase. In other words we, like the classical jurists, have been misled by the later usage of the word *emo* and have supported our misuse by anthropological theory.

Of course, the presence of the scales or balances and five witnesses lends some plausibility to the theory that this was in origin a sale, even though the sale-formula was not used and apparently no coin passed. However, I take it that in the early days, before writing was known, some symbolic act that could be witnessed and remembered was desirable in making contracts. The symbol of the balances was, of course, frequently used in making purchases and might well have spread from that act to all other contracts that had to be witnessed. It came also to be used in such contracts as *nexum*, in the adoption of children, and in the making of wills,[17] though in these cases it did not imply purchase. Gaius, for instance, says that in ancient times when a man was sick and expected death he would call the person he desired to be his heir, give him his instructions and his property, and the latter, in the presence of five witnesses, would verbally accept the willed property, strike the scales, and hand the piece of bronze to the testator. He adds that this had become by his day the usual formality in making wills. Now it seems to me difficult to hold that the heir actually bought the property with the penny, for which the dying testator had no use, or that the penny represented an actual payment to be made later. This act probably never represented a sale; it was a convenient formality for the five witnesses to behold and could be readily remembered. The shaking of hands before witnesses would have served the same purpose, had it become the custom.[18] The symbolism was clearly borrowed from one kind of contract to be used in another because before the day of writing a common formality that could be seen and recalled was needed.

I would also suggest, though with some diffidence, that when this ceremony was used in adoption — as when Augustus metamorphosed his two grandsons into sons [19] — we may be wrong in assuming that he "bought" them from his son-in-law, Agrippa. The *mancipatio* in this case may have meant only a transfer of *manus* and the ceremony may simply have been a visible symbol of the transfer used because it could easily be remembered by the witnesses. In other words, when *coemptio* is employed in adoption, it need not be a *survival* of a rite that once meant purchase in that very transaction; it may represent merely the diffusion of a useful rite originally employed in an act of purchase. Of course, the use of the words *emancipatio* and *coemptio* with reference to children led later lawyers to suppose that children were property like slaves, but it is not certain that this supposition did not rest upon ideas that arose after the words had passed through several semantic changes and no longer possessed their original meanings.

Karlowa,[20] imbued with the idea that the coemptive formula used in marriage must have implied purchase, has invented a convenient phrase and persuaded many writers to insert it into the formula. He proposed to emend the words cited by Gellius (IV, 3) as follows: *Te ego ex jure Quiritium in manu mancipioque meo esse aio tuque mihi coempta esto.* However, this proposed emendation on the analogy of the sale-formula is wholly inconsonant with the mutual questions and answers cited by Ulpian, with the statement of Gaius [21] that the formula and purport of coemptive marriage differed from that of a sale, with the fact that Cicero [22] (*ejus mulieris quae coemptionem fecerit*) and Gaius (I, 114, *potest autem coemptionem facere mulier*, etc.) speak at times of the woman as the one who *facit coemptionem*, and with the fact that Servius [23] speaks of *coemptio* as a mutual transfer. If we forget anthropological comparisons with savage customs of bride-purchase for a while, and conceive of the symbolic rite of coemptive marriage as simply borrowed from the formalities used in sales, testaments, adoption, nexum, and the like, that is, as a convenient method of employing witnesses to observe the striking of the contract, we shall have no difficulty with our sources. There is no mention of a piece of bronze, probably because none passed; the act of *coemptio* is spoken of at times as being *mutual*, or when convenient, the *mulier* or the *vir* may be spoken of as performing a *coemptio*, because in this contract the give and take was equal; it was not one-sided. At times, since in this old form of marriage the bride passed from the *manus* of the father to the husband, the word *mancipio* is used, but not in the sense of a sale, as Gaius is careful to say, but only in the literal sense of *manus*-acceptance. And, finally, the formula used was different from that of a contract of sale, because it had nothing whatsoever to do with sales. Only the paraphernalia were similar, and those only because they were so much in use in other contracts made before the day of writing that they were generally accessible. It is only fair to concede that this interpretation of *coemptio* is not hereby definitely established. However, in view of the many difficulties into which the older opinions have led jurists, it seemed to me urgent to reopen the discussion by offering a solution that seemed rather to accord with the known facts.

These few examples will perhaps suffice to indicate the source of my belief that, if the students of law will read the newer economic and social histories of Rome based upon the results of recent excavations, they will find reason to give a more patient consideration to various neglected fragments of the Twelve Tables and will arrive at a more reasonable interpretation of the contractual ceremonies described in them. A new school of jurists has recently emerged which is advocating the study of sociology and economics in order to release the interpretation of present-day law from outworn tradition. It is also necessary, it seems to me, that students of ancient law should make a careful investigation of the social and economic conditions out of which the law grew before they undertake to explain the meaning and intention of the phrases that they attempt to interpret.

NOTES

CHAPTER I

1. Levy, *Der Hergang der röm. Ehescheidung* (1925), p. 45, has shown that the seven witnesses required by the Julian law were necessary only when by this law a husband was required to divorce an unfaithful wife. For the laws on Roman matrimony and divorce see art. "Matrimonium" by Kunkel in Pauly-Wissowa XIV, 2260, and Corbett, *The Roman Law of Marriage*, 1930. The passage from Cicero occurs in *Ad Fam.* 8, 7.

2. *Pro Murena* 27. Even in Cato's day women kept their own property after marriage; see Malcovati *Oratorum Rom. Frag.* I, p. 190. In Chapter V the meaning of *coemptio* is discussed. Apparently there is no sure trace of bride-purchase in Rome.

3. On divorce, see Levy, *op. cit.*

4. In Cic. *Ad Att.* 15, 11.

5. Cf. Plutarch, *Cato*, 20, and *Aemilius Paulus*, 6. On Cicero see *Ad Att.* 8, 4, 1; Nepos, *Atticus*, 1, 2, has something to say on home-instruction. The passage in Tacitus is *Dialogus*, 28.

6. On the social legislation of Augustus see Corbett, *The Roman Law of Marriage*, pp. 31–39, 119–121, 133–135.

7. Frank, *Life and Literature in the Roman Republic*, chaps. iii and iv.

8. Münzer, *Röm. Adelsparteien*, p. 272.

CHAPTER II

1. W. Warde Fowler has well described the old Roman religion in *The Religious Experience of the Roman People*; see especially chaps. viii, ix, and xix. For the new religions of the Empire see Cumont, *Les Religions orientales dans le paganisme romain* (4th ed., 1929), with its excellent bibliography.

2. Toutain, *Les Cultes païens dans l'empire romain* (1907–20). His study of the Oriental cults in the western provinces appears in Vol. II (1922). My study of *Race Mixture in the Roman Empire* appeared in the *Am. Hist. Rev.* (1916), pp. 689–708. La Piana's *Foreign Groups in Rome during the first centuries of the Empire* is to be found in *Harvard Theol. Rev.* (1927), pp. 183–403.

3. Anthropology, which has employed cranial measurements in the study of European "races," has pursued an incorrect theory of evolution. The mixture of races physically different took place so many scores of millennia ago that physical criteria have little significance in European history. Racial differences that may be of some value in early historical study are those of temperament, and these arose by processes of selection here and there during the few thousand years when men were first taking to agriculture and close habitation.

4. *Op. cit.*, *Am. Hist. Rev.* (1916); cf. M. E. Park, *The Plebs in Cicero's Day* (1918), who has given lists especially of military losses, and of war captives. In the *Cambridge Ancient History*, VIII (1930), 335 ff., I have discussed the introduction of slave-economy into Italy.

5. A confused account of the incident is given in Livy 39, 8–13. For my attempt to explain it, see *Class. Quart.* (1927), p. 128. Cumont, *op. cit.*, pp. 197 ff., has traced the later history of the cult at Rome.

6. Greek-speaking freedmen were largely employed as agents by Roman merchants when their commerce expanded eastward after the Gracchan period. The Alexandrian merchants were then very powerful on the eastern seas and especially at Delos, the favorite eastern port of exchange in the Aegean. Furthermore the Egyptian king visited Sulla at Rome in 81 B.C. If it is true that there were worshippers of Isis at Rome in Sulla's day, we may presume that they were Alexandrians closely connected with these events. Later (in 59) when Caesar exacted large sums from Ptolemy Auletes in return for his support and placed Rabirius in charge of the Egyptian monopolies in order to collect the revenues of Egypt to secure the amounts due, a large part of the Alexandrian shipping was deflected to Rome's harbors. In 59 Ptolemy, with a large retinue, lived at Rome for several months. These facts will account for the references to Isis worship at Rome in the years 54–48 B.C. Cleopatra came to Rome in 45 and departed after Caesar's death. The shrine at Rome was ordered built by the Senate in 43 (Cass. Dio 47, 15).

7. See Cumont, *Les Religions Orientales*, chap. iv.

8. In the early Empire several important scholars of Alexandria, like Chairemon, the tutor of Nero, served as teachers, librarians, and civil servants at Rome.

9. Toutain, *op. cit.*, Vol. II, chap. i. Evidence of the presence of the Isiac cult is found in 19 places in Africa, 15 in Spain, 15 in Narbonese Gaul, 10 along the Rhine, 20 in Pannonia, 13 in Dacia, and at a few other points, according to Toutain. He concludes his study with the remark that in the West the Isiac cult remained wholly exotic (p. 34). Cumont has criticized this conclusion as based too largely upon inscriptional evidence (*Rev. hist. rel.* [1912], 125) preferring rather to rely upon literary documents like the *Metamorphoses* of Apuleius; but Apuleius was himself an immigrant from Africa where the Isiac cult had followed a vigorous Alexandrian trade.

10. Carcopino, *Attideia*, in *Mél. d'Arch. et d'Hist.* (1923), pp. 135–159.

11. Cheesman, *The Auxilia of the Roman Army*, p. 84. For the movements of the legions see Ritterling, *Legio* in Pauly-Wissowa. For the distribution of the worshippers especially in the army see Toutain, *op. cit.*, Vol. II, chap. iv.

12. See *Race Mixture*, in *Am. Hist. Rev.* (1916), pp. 689–708. Among those of servile origin we must reckon the imperial freedmen who assumed the nomen of an emperor (Aelius, Flavius, etc.) and *liberti* who shaped a nomen from a town or gild (Ostiensis, Publicius, Centonius, etc.).

13. These have been discussed by Rostovtzeff, in his *Mystic Italy*.

14. See my *Life and Literature in the Roman Republic* (1930), p. 220.

15. This seems to be true of the brilliant works of Carcopino: *La Basilique Pythagoricienne* (1927), and *Virgile et la mistère de la IVe Eclogue* (1930).

16. Kittel, *Die hellenistische Myst. und des Alte Test.* (1924).

17. Clemen, in *Relig. Versuche und Vorarbeiten* (1913), goes perhaps too far toward rejecting this influence, but his criticism of current views is timely.

CHAPTER III

1. For recent discussions of Roman rural society see Heitland, *Agricola*, 151 ff.; Pöhlmann-Oertel, *Geschichte d. soz. Frage* (3rd ed., 1925); Rostovtzeff, *The Social and Economic History of the Roman Empire*; M. Weber, *Röm. Agrargeschichte*; Kromayer, *Die*

wirtschaftl. Entwicklung Italiens, in *Neue Jahrb.* (1914), pp. 145 ff.; Gummerus, *Der röm. Gutsbetrieb*, Klio, Beiheft 6 (1906); Frank, in *Cambridge Ancient History*, VIII, 333–383; Toutain, *L'Economie Antique*, pp. 334 ff.

2. See *Am. Journal Philology* (1930), pp. 313 ff.

3. The Lex Fannia. Pliny, *H. N.* X, 71, gives the date as 161; cf. Macrobius III, 17, 4, and Gellius II, 24. The references in Polybius to the financial affairs of the younger Scipio are XVIII, 35, and XXXII, 12–14.

4. Kromayer, in *Neue Jahrb.* (1914), pp. 145 ff.

5. Typical references to farmers; Cato, *Agric.*, preface; Varro, *De Re Rust.* I, 2, 12; Cic. *Cato major*, 51; *De Off.* II, 12; Vergil, *Georgics*, II, 459; Tibullus I, 7 and II, 1. Less complimentary: Cic. *Pro Sext. Rosc.* 74; *Phil.* II, 33; *Leg. Agr.* II, 95; *Pro Cael.* 36; *De Orat.* I, 115; *Orator*, 148; *Brutus*, 286.

6. For instance, very few, if any, of the literary men of Rome were born in the capital. Most of them came from farms or from small towns whose citizens were in the main landowners. The list of these includes Naevius, Ennius, Plautus, Lucilius, Catullus (with the whole Cisalpine group: Valerius Cato, Varius Rufus, Cinna, etc.), Cicero, Vergil, Horace, Propertius, Ovid, Tibullus, Lucan, Seneca, Pliny, etc. As in America, where distinguished men (recorded, for instance, in *Who's Who*), even when born on farms, are generally credited to the towns that have the nearest post-office address, so in Italy farmers gave as their place of nativity the town where their registration was recorded. Vergil, for instance, reckoned as a Mantuan though he was born on a farm three miles away from Mantua.

7. For the politics of this period see *Cambridge Ancient History*, Vol. VIII.

8. See *Roman Census Statistics*, Class. Phil. (1924), pp. 335 ff., and Sallust, *Hist.*, *Oratio Lepidi*, 12.

9. Cic. *Cat.* II, 20.

10. Cic. *Ad Att.* 7, 7, 5.

11. The so-called "Lex Julia Municipalis," Dessau, *I. L. S.* 6085, 142 ff.

12. Rostovtzeff gives a useful list of these in his *Soc. and Econ. History*, p. 496.

13. De Pachtere, *La Table Hypoth. de Veleia*, an excellent study.

14. Rostovtzeff has well described the debacle of that period, *op. cit.*, pp. 381–410.

15. See N. H. Baynes, in *Jour. Rom. Stud.* (1929), p. 229.

CHAPTER IV

1. On Roman marriage see Corbett, *The Roman Law of Marriage*, and Chapter V in this volume.

2. Cf. *Cambridge Ancient History*, Vol. VIII, chaps. x and xi. So long as the family met its natural obligations there was little need for such charitable institutions as asylums for the aged.

3. I have discussed this aspect in *An Economic History of Rome* (2nd ed.), pp. 418 ff., making liberal use of the valuable investigations of De Pachtere, *La Table Hypoth. de Veleia* (Paris, 1920).

4. The only instance of state intervention spoken of in favor of commerce or agriculture was the prohibition of wine-raising among the hills of Savoy. But this prohibition, occurring in a treaty signed jointly by Marseilles and Rome, was laid down in favor of Marseilles, and fell in abeyance when Marseilles lost her control over the neighborhood. See my *Economic History* (2nd ed.), pp. 116–117.

5. See the excellent chapters on Rome under the Flavians and Antonines in Rostovtzeff, *Social and Economic History*, pp. 180–343.

6. Cicero, *De Republica*, III, 22; though the *De Republica* was lost, this passage survived in a quotation by Lactantius and thus spread into medieval and eighteenth-century books.

7. Mommsen was mistaken in assuming that Roman jurists of the Republic considered the provinces Roman public property; cf. *Jour. Roman Studies* (1927), pp. 141–161.

8. The recent theory that the Roman emperors frequently intervened in favor of urbanization in the provinces during the first two centuries of the Empire finds little support in our sources. The emperors built many good *military* roads and suppressed brigandage; as a natural consequence trade and industry flourished and cities sprang up along the trade routes; then the emperors naturally concentrated their gifts of public funds where the greater number could enjoy them.

9. See Chapter II.

CHAPTER V

1. See L. Wenger, *Der heutige Stand der röm. Rechtswissenschaft* (1927). A part of this chapter appeared in *Proc. Am. Philos. Soc.* LXX, 193 ff.

2. Male carmen, Tab. VIII, 1 a. (Bruns-Gradenwitz). See Huvelin, *La notion de l'injuria*; Kübler, *Gesch. des röm. Rechts*, p. 52.

3. Tab. III, 6; see Radin, in *Am. Jour. Phil.* (1922), p. 32.

4. I attempted in my *Economic History of Rome* (1920), pp. 13 ff. (2nd ed., 1927), to present the results of recent excavations on these points; see also Tamborini, *La vita economica*, in Athenaeum (1930), pp. 299 f.

5. I use Bruns-Gradenwitz for the text and wish to refer especially to Girard, *Manuel* (5th ed.), Kübler, *Geschichte des röm. Rechts*, and Radin, *Handbook of Roman Law*, for standard discussions and bibliographies.

6. Venditae vero et traditae (res) non aliter emptori adquiruntur quam si is venditori pretium solverit *vel alio modo satisfecerit, veluti expromissore aut pignore dato*; quod cavetur quidem etiam lege XII tabularum.

7. Varro, *L. L.* V, 163.

8. For the first treaty with Carthage see Polybius III, 22 (cf. my *Econ. Hist. of Rome* [1927], p. 34); the Cassian treaty is found in Dionys. VI, 95.

9. Kübler, *Geschichte des röm. Rechts*, p. 55. The same author has discussed (in *Zeitschrift Savig. Stift.* [1920], p. 43) the very liberal provision in the Twelve Tables whereby daughters inherited on the same footing as sons in case of intestacy.

10. Leonhard, *familia* in Pauly-Wissowa; see also Thes. *L. L.* on *familia*. According to Walde, *Lat. etym. Wörterbuch*, the root of the word seems to be a cognate of Skr. *dhaman* and of Θαιμός = dwelling.

11. Pomponius, *Dig.* 50, 16, 120. Cf. Gaius, II, 224. This important passage is not even quoted (though referred to) in Bruns-Gradenwitz; and Kübler, *Gesch. röm. Rechts*, p. 58, adds that few now believe that there was *Testierfreiheit*. See, however, Manigk on *hereditarium jus* in Pauly-Wissowa, who interprets the passage more liberally.

12. This trend seems also to explain the custom of leaving the estate undivided, so that one son might buy out the other heirs and keep the estate intact. The provision of *familiae erciscundae* was mentioned in the Twelve Tables (Tab. V, 10), so that the custom must have been an old one.

13. See Corbett, *The Roman Law of Marriage*, and Kunkel, *Matrimonium*, in Pauly-Wissowa XIV, 2260.

14. Cicero, *De Oratore* I, 237: ejus mulieris quae coemptionem fecerit, *Pro Murena* 27: mulieres quae coemptionem facerent 'Gaias' vocari. Cf. Gaius I, 114 and 123, and Servius on Vergil, *Georg.* I, 31.

15. Gaius I, 123, quod non similiter fit in coemptione.

16. Boethius, *Topica* 3.

17. Festus, 160 L; Gellius, XV, 27; Suet. *Aug.* 64; Gaius II, 102.

18. The plausible suggestion has been made by Beseler (*Zeitschr. Sav. St.* 45, 428) that *mancipatio* originally meant handshake. The shaking of hands over bargains was apparently not used at Rome in historical times, and perhaps the formula *per aes et libram* took its place. We are still in doubt about the original meaning of *mancipatio*: see Kunkel, *sub. voc.* in Pauly-Wissowa XIV, 1007.

19. Suet. *Aug.* 64.

20. *Rechtsgeschichte* II, 161.

21. Gaius, I, 123.

22. See note 14.

23. On Vergil, *Georg.* I, 31.

INDEX

INDEX